Never Send
a Human to Do
a Machine's Job

Never Send a Human to Do a Machine's Job

Correcting the Top 5 EdTech Mistakes

Yong Zhao

Gaoming Zhang

Jing Lei

Wei Qiu

CORWIN
A SAGE Company

A SAGE Company

FOR INFORMATION:

Corwin

A SAGE Company

2455 Teller Road

Thousand Oaks, California 91320

(800) 233-9936

www.corwin.com

SAGE Publications Ltd.

1 Oliver's Yard

55 City Road

London EC1Y 1SP

United Kingdom

SAGE Publications India Pvt. Ltd.

B 1/I 1 Mohan Cooperative Industrial Area

Mathura Road, New Delhi 110 044

India

SAGE Publications Asia-Pacific Pte. Ltd.

3 Church Street

#10-04 Samsung Hub

Singapore 049483

Printed in the United States of America

ISBN 978-1-4522-8257-2

This book is printed on acid-free paper.

Executive Editor: Arnis Burvikovs

Associate Editor: Ariel Price

Editorial Assistant: Andrew Olson

Production Editor: Amy Schroller

Copy Editor: Sarah J. Duffy

Typesetter: C&M Digitals (P) Ltd.

Proofreader: Susan Schon

Indexer: Sheila Bodell

Cover Designer: Gail Buschman

Marketing Manager: Amy Vader

Certified Chain of Custody
Promoting Sustainable Forestry
www.sfiprogram.org
SFI-01268

SUSTAINABLE FORESTRY INITIATIVE

SFI label applies to text stock

15 16 17 18 19 10 9 8 7 6 5 4 3 2 1

Contents

Acknowledgments

Corwin gratefully acknowledges the contributions of the following reviewers:

Chris Hubbuch
Principal
Excelsior Springs Middle School
Excelsior Springs, MO

Loukea Kovanis-Wilson
Chemistry Teacher
Clarkston High School
Clarkston, MI

Tina Kuchinski
English Teacher and Department Chair
Gresham High School
Gresham, OR

Ernie Rambo
Educator
Walter Johnson Junior High School
Las Vegas, NV

About the Authors

 Yong Zhao currently serves as the Presidential Chair and Director of the Institute for Global and Online Education in the College of Education, University of Oregon, where he is also a Professor in the Department of Educational Measurement, Policy, and Leadership. He is also a professorial fellow at the Mitchell Institute for Health and Education Policy, Victoria University. His works focus on the implications of globalization and technology on education. He has published over 100 articles and 20 books, including *Who's Afraid of the Big Bad Dragon: Why China Has the Best (and Worst) Education System in the World, Catching Up or Leading the Way: American Education in the Age of Globalization,* and *World Class Learners: Educating Creative and Entrepreneurial Students.* He is a recipient of the Early Career Award from the American Educational Research Association and was named one of 2012"s 10 most influential people in educational technology by the Tech & Learn Magazine. He is an elected fellow of the International Academy for Education. His latest book *World Class Learners* has won several awards including the Society of Professors of Education Book Award (2013), Association of Education Publishers' (AEP) Judges' Award and Distinguished Achievement Award in Education Leadership (2013).

Gaoming Zhang is an Assistant Professor in the School of Education at the University of Indianapolis. She teaches educational psychology and educational technology courses in undergraduate and graduate programs. Her research interests include technology integration, teacher preparation, and comparative education. Her work has appeared in *On the Horizon*, the *Journal of Early Childhood Teacher Education*, *Asia Pacific Journal of Education*, *Educause Review*, and *The International Encyclopedia of Education*.

Jing Lei is an Associate Professor in the School of Education at Syracuse University. Dr. Lei's scholarship focuses on how information and communication technology can help prepare a new generation of citizens for a globalizing and digitizing world. Specifically, her research interests include technology integration in schools, the social-cultural and psychological impact of technology, e-learning, emerging technologies for education, and teacher technology preparation. Her recent publications include *Handbook of Asian Education: A Cultural Perspective* (2011, Routledge) and *The Digital Pencil: One-to-One Computing for Children* (2008, Lawrence Erlbaum Associates).

Wei Qiu is an instructional designer and adjunct faculty at Webster University. She received a PhD in Educational Psychology and Educational Technology from Michigan State University. Her research interests include using technology to enhance students' learning experience, second language education, and global competency development.

Introduction

Cyclic amnesia best characterizes the history of technology in education. Over the last 100 years or so, we have gone through many cycles of hope and then disappointment: from film to radio, from radio to TV, from TV to computers, and from computers to the Internet. Every cycle started with amazing euphoria and then ended with disappointing outcomes. But somehow, we managed to forget the failures. We did not even stop to reflect what went wrong because new technology emerged, with more power and thus more hope. The new technology seemed so compelling that we could not afford time to reflect. We must act quickly to realize the potential of the new technology. Otherwise, we'd be missing out on its educational benefits. As a result, we have been repeating the same mistakes. I have suffered from amnesia as well, but would like to change that. Hence this book.

I have been very disappointed with the effects of technology on education. Despite the powerful potential of technology and massive investment in technology for educational purposes, the impact on education has been extremely limited. Technology has not solved many significant educational problems on a large scale. The *deus ex machina* in education has never appeared. This is a depressing realization after 30 years of attempts to improve learning through technology.

In 1985, I tried to use the Apple II to teach English vocabulary when I was in college in China. I had imagined that computerized programs would help everyone master the English language a lot faster. My program did not go very far. Other than me, nobody else used it. Although I learned a lot of English words through programming, the benefits did not come from using the software. Instead they came from programming.

I was an amateur, but there were numerous professionals and businesses designing software and technology systems for language learning at the time. A field called computer-assisted language learning (CALL) evolved, with professional organizations, professional journals, and conferences. Schools purchased computers and built language labs. But today students all over the world still struggle to learn languages, and most of them learn from human teachers.

Ten years later, in 1995, I began using the Internet to teach foreign languages at the college level. With the powerful capacity to connect teachers and students from all over the world and easy access to original language and cultural resources, the Information Highway, as it was popularly known then, was going to deliver a revolution in language learning.

"Motivation" thus became my answer to a question posed to me by Professor Patrick Dickson of Michigan State University. He chaired the search committee that hired me as an assistant professor in educational technology. Patrick asked this question during my job interview in 1995: "In 10 years, what would be the reason if most people in the world are not bilingual given the potentials of the Internet for language learning?"

Today, most people in the world remain monolingual, and motivation may be only part of the reason. By and large, students of foreign languages continue to learn the same old way: a human teacher, textbooks, and exercise sheets. Very few students actually make use of the native speakers available online or the vast amount of newspapers, books, TV shows, and YouTube videos to learn the target language. As a result, 2 years of high school Spanish still does not give many students the capacity to function in the language.

Another 10 years passed. In 2005, I was designing an online computer game to teach Chinese to kids all over the world. Computer games have been found to be addictive, so they should be more engaging to children. Online social games have been extremely popular among young people. With increased bandwidth, enhanced graphics, and virtually ubiquitous access to computers, a massively multiplayer online role-playing game (MMORPG) would drastically improve the effectiveness of learning language. So I thought. The game was developed and piloted. There were many users. However, the fact remains that after a decade, Chinese language is still learned virtually the same way it was done in the 1960s or perhaps 1800s: human teachers and textbooks.

In 2015, efforts to develop and deploy technological solutions for language learning continue. But I am much less enthusiastic about its revolutionary outcomes as I was 10, 20, or 30 years ago, when the technology was much less powerful.

I have been repeatedly disappointed by my own efforts to bring about more effective education through technology. My personal disappointing journey is, unfortunately, not an isolated case. In fact, the failure of technology to deliver its grand promise to transform education is not even isolated to the field of language learning. It is repeated in all fields of education: math, social studies, science, and other subjects. There have been high hopes and diligent efforts in all areas. There have been exemplary pockets of success. But by and large, technology has not done much to improve education on a large scale. In the big picture, students' academic performance has remained flat over the last several decades, as measured by the National Assessment of Educational Progress and other historical assessments. The achievement gap has persisted.

This is not because we were mistaken about the power of modern information and communication technology. There is no doubt that computers are much more powerful than paper or even people in handling certain types of information and carrying out certain tasks. More important, technology keeps getting more powerful and less expensive. Over the past 30 years, digital technology has become increasingly sophisticated and omnipresent. It has transformed virtually all aspects of our lives. It has displaced workers in traditional professions. It has made entire lines of jobs disappear. It has created new mega companies and millions of new jobs. It has changed how we live, entertain, travel, work, and socialize. But it has not fundamentally transformed education, despite the emergence of online schools, massively open online courses (MOOCs), and introduction of technological devices into classrooms.

It is not due to lack of effort, either. Enormous amounts of money have been spent to equip schools. In 1995 the dream plan for a revolution was to have a student-to-computer ratio of 5:1. That was realized. Then we wanted 1:1, student to laptop, and that has become a reality in many schools. Virtually all schools and classrooms are connected today—a tremendous journey and investment to move from nothing to dial-up connection, to ISDN, to cable, to fiber optic, and to wireless. Computer labs have become a necessary feature of all schools.

There have also been tremendous efforts to prepare teachers and school leaders. Technology proficiency standards have been created and added for teacher certification or recertification. Professional development programs have been offered to in-service teachers. Educational technology courses have been added to teacher education programs for preservice teachers. Graduate degree programs have been developed and provided to technology leaders in schools. Professional organizations, publications, and conferences in educational technology have multiplied over the past 30 years.

Efforts to develop educational technology products and services have been undertaken by education practitioners, researchers, and businesses. Governments have provided funds in support of innovations in educational technology as well. Numerous innovative products have been developed. The educational technology market in the U.S. preK–12 sector has grown to nearly $10 billion, which can buy a lot of products and services.

Why hasn't technology transformed education as much as it has transformed other sectors? And more important, what can be done to realize its transformative power in education? In this book, my coauthors and I attempt to point out the reasons and suggest a new approach to using technology to better prepare our children for the future.

We took a retrospective review of past efforts to use technology in education, and we discovered that they have not been transformative largely because of five mistaken approaches. First, we have applied a misconstrued relationship between teachers and technology. Traditionally, technology has been viewed as something to either replace the teacher or aid the teacher, which directed efforts to develop products and services to replace the human teacher entirely or tools for teachers to use. A more productive relationship may be in the middle. That is, technology can replace certain functions of the human teacher, but not entirely. In the meantime, teachers do not need to control technology as simply a teaching tool to enhance instruction. Instead they should relinquish some of their teaching responsibilities to technology and shift their energy to do things that technology cannot do. This calls for a reconceptualization of the relationship as a partnership between teachers and technology.

The second mistaken approach is the way technology is treated in schools in relation to students. The traditional approach has been to use technology to help students "consume" information more effectively. It has been used mainly as a way to help students learn better the existing curriculum, while a much more productive way is to help students use technology as a tool for creating and making authentic products. This calls for a transformation in how we view student learning.

The third mistaken approach is the result of our erroneous expectations and definition of educational outcomes. With the increasing pressure on schools to improve student academic achievement, often measured by standardized tests, investment in technology has historically been justified as an effective way to raise academic results or test scores. Thus technology has often been limited in traditional instructional practices instead of viewed as a transformative tool to create better education for all students.

The fourth set of mistakes is derived from the wrong assumption that technology is there only to improve existing curriculum and instruction while neglecting the fact that technology has created a new world, which demands new skills and knowledge. In other words, traditional approaches to educational technology have not typically viewed digital competence or the ability to live in the digital age as legitimate educational outcomes. Consequently, not much attention has been given to transforming schools into environments that cultivate digital competence.

The final mistake is the approach to professional development of educators. Too often professional development efforts have been driven by technological products instead of the needs of students and educational change. Technology changes fast. New products and services come out all the time at nonstop speed. To help teachers make use of technology, many professional development programs have been developed in schools. These programs often have a focus on teaching teachers how to use the newest technological tools instead of focusing on what students need and how technology as a whole can affect education.

The first five chapters of the book are devoted to each of the mistakes we have made. We illustrate these mistakes with stories and examples, research-based evidence, and provocative questions. But our purpose in writing this book is not limited to exposing the mistakes. Rather, it is to suggest a new way of thinking about technology in education, which we do in Chapter 6.

A new way to think about technology and education is "never send a human to do a machine's job," advice from Agent Smith in the film *The Matrix*. In education, we need to redefine the relationship between humans and machines based on thoughtful analyses of what humans do best and what should be relegated to technology. There is no reason to have human teachers do things that machines do better or more effectively. There is no reason to have human teachers perform routine, mechanical, and boring tasks when technology can do. After all, the reason to have technology is to extend, expand, and/or replace certain human functions.

The redefinition of relationship can only happen when we begin to reimagine what education should be like. Thus in Chapter 6 we outline a series of possible changes that should and can happen to achieve better educational outcomes, not necessarily in order to simply use technology more. Technology has made it both a necessity and a possibility to realize some of the long-standing proposals for child-centered education and learning by doing. Personalized education that grants students autonomy and respects their uniqueness has become a necessity for cultivating the abilities required for living in a society when machines are rapidly taking jobs away from humans. Technology has made it possible to enable personalized learning and to have students take more control of their own learning. Moreover, technology has also made it possible for students to engage in authentic learning by tackling real-world problems on a global scale.

In summary, technology has been traditionally conceived as a tool to enhance and improve existing practices within the existing educational setup, but it has become a tool to enable a grand education transformation that has been imagined by many pioneering thinkers such John Dewey. The transformation is not about technology, but about more meaningful education for all children. Perhaps finally we can escape the cyclic amnesia we have suffered in using technology to improve education.

This book is a review of what happened in the past. It is intended to challenge traditional thinking, practices, and policies. More important, it is intended to stimulate new thinking about the future of education and technology. Thus, while we criticize past-oriented practices and policies, we also provide numerous examples of emerging future-oriented practices and programs that reflect new ways of thinking. It is our hope that this book can help school leaders, policymakers, teachers, and parents reimagine education in the digital age.

The book is a collaborative project. The coauthors have been working together on issues discussed in this book for about a decade. During the process of writing, Gaoming Zhang took the lead to develop the proposal and helped coordinate the effort. While each chapter has a lead author (Chapters 1 and 3 by Gaoming Zhang, Chapters 2 and 4 by Jing Lei, Chapter 5 by Wei Qiu, and Chapter 6 by Yong Zhao), all authors reviewed and contributed to all the chapters. I am grateful for the work of the entire team.

—*Yong Zhao*

April 2015

CHAPTER ONE

The Wrong Relationship Between Technology and Teachers

Complementing in an Ecosystem Versus Replacing in a Hierarchy

Will classroom TV replace teachers?

James Montagnes raised this question in his article that appeared in the *Eugene Register-Guard* on December 16, 1954. The question was very timely since the 1950s was a time of unprecedented development of television. The percentage of American homes that had television sets jumped dramatically from 5% in 1950 to 87% in the end of the 1950s (Sterling & Kittross, 1990). In his article, Montagnes reported a large-scale experiment in Canada in which fifth, sixth, seventh, and eighth graders in 200 schools watched TV programs on current events, history, art, science, safety, and literature. An example of a televised lesson was "How Columbus Navigated." This 20-minute film showed the actual types of instruments Columbus used for his trip and how he demonstrated to the crew that he knew he wasn't lost. Montagnes's article concluded with the prediction that "the day will come when video is as commonplace in schools as erasers and blackboards." At the end of the article, Montagnes asked a perplexing question: "Will TV receivers in classrooms change the role of the teacher and someday largely replace her?"

Since then James Montagnes's question of about whether teachers will be replaced has been revisited from time to time. Every time when there is a major technology innovation that holds great potential in teaching and learning, this question is raised again. The prevalence of computers in schools brought probably the most heated debate on the topic. In the 1990s President Bill Clinton campaigned for "a bridge to the twenty-first century . . . where computers are as much a part of the classroom as blackboards" (quoted in Oppenheimer, 1997). And two decades later, that became the reality. By 2009, approximately 97% of teachers in the United States had at least one computer in the classroom every day and 54% could bring computers into the classroom (Gray, Thomas, Lewis, & Tice, 2010). Internet access also became widely accessible, available for 93% of computers located in the classroom every day and for 96% of computers that could be brought into the classroom. Also by 2009, the ratio of students to computers in the classroom every day was 5.3 to 1 (Gray et al., 2010). As a result, variations on Montagnes's question made more headlines: "Quality Debated as Districts Tap Tech Over Teachers" from *Education Week* (Quillen, 2012), "Can Computers Replace Teachers?" from *TIME Ideas* (Rotherham, 2012), and "Can Computers Take the Place of teachers?" from *CNN Opinion* (Mitra, 2010).

Very soon, online education became the next target of the question as it was the fastest-growing segment of education (Allen & Seaman, 2011). According to a recent report on online education in the United States, over 6.1 million students took at least one online course during the fall 2010 term, an increase of 560,000 students over the previous year (Allen & Seaman, 2011). In addition, the 10% growth rate for online enrollments far exceeds the average 2% growth in the overall higher education student population. The most recent version of the question is "Can tablets replace teachers?" ("Digital Schools," 2013).

So here are different generations of James Montagnes's question, and new versions will likely arise when we experience new technology innovations.

Will TV replace teachers?

Will computers replace teachers?

Will online education replace teachers?

Will tablets replace teachers?

While these questions focus on a particular technology that became prevalent in classrooms and seemed promising for teaching and learning, the essence of such questions remains the same: What is the relationship between technology (e.g., TV, computers, the Internet, tablets) and teachers? Does (or can) technology fully assume teachers' responsibilities, as various versions of the question "Will teachers be replaced?" suggest?

AN ECOSYSTEM, NOT A HIERARCHY: RECONSIDERING THE RELATIONSHIP BETWEEN TEACHERS AND TECHNOLOGY

A Hierarchy: Displacement Theory and Media Comparison Studies

These questions illustrate well the displacement theory and media comparison studies, both of which view the relationship between media (i.e., all kinds of technology and teachers) as a hierarchy. The hierarchy mindset is committed to finding out which medium is the best.

The primary interests of the displacement theory are "Is B better than A?" and "Can B replace A?" Here B represents a new medium (e.g., radio, television, computers, the Internet) while A is the existing medium. When a new medium is acquired, people who embrace the displacement theory would label the new medium as a threat to the existing medium. They are eager to find out which one is better. Research that is guided by the displacement theory tends to conduct head-to-head comparison between a new type of educational technology and the existing medium, such as between radio and newspaper

(Lazarsfeld, 1940; Mendelsohn, 1964), between television and news-papers/magazines/radio (Belson, 1961; E. Rubenstein et al., 1973; Williams, 1986), and recently between computers and the Internet (Althaus & Tewksbury, 2000; Finholt & Sproull, 1990; Kayany & Yelsma, 2000; Kaye & Johnson, 2003).

By the same token, the pressing questions of media comparison studies are "Is B (e.g., a new educational technology) better than teachers?" and "Can B (e.g., a new educational technology) replace teachers?" These two questions serve as the template for different versions of James Montagnes's question. A large body of research has been conducted in an attempt to answer these two questions (see meta-analyses by Cohen, Ebling, & Kulik, 1981; C. Kulik, Kulik, & Cohen, 1980; J. Kulik, Bangert, & Williams, 1983; J. Kulik, Kulik, & Cohen, 1979). A typical study would compare the achievement of participants who learn from different media. A recent example is a study by the U.S. Department of Education on the effectiveness of reading and mathematics software products (National Center for Education Evaluation and Regional Assistance, 2007). The study compared student achievement in four groups between the class-rooms that used the technology products and traditional classrooms that did not. The four groups were reading in first and fourth grades, mathematics in sixth grade, and high school algebra (National Center for Education Evaluation and Regional Assistance, 2007).

Both displacement theory and media comparison studies are driven by an assumption that media are a hierarchy and that we have to rank media to find out which is better in instruction. However, consistent and strong evidence has found that there are no learning benefits from just employing a specific medium to deliver instruc-tion, from the radio research in the 1950s (e.g., Hovland, Lumsdaine, & Sheffield, 1949), to the television movement of the 1960s (e.g., Schramm, Lyle, & Parker, 1961), to the computer-assisted instruc-tion studies in the 1970s and 1980s (e.g., Dixon & Judd, 1977). In his comprehensive review of media comparison studies, Richard E. Clark (1983) concludes, "Five decades of research suggest that there are no learning benefits to be gained from employing different media in instruction, regardless of their obviously attractive features or advertised superiority" (p. 450). Repeated comparison of face-to-face education and Web-based instruction seems to lead to the same con-clusion. Recent results from Bernard et al. (2004) and other reviews of the distance education literature (Cavanaugh, 2001; Moore, 1994) indicate no significant differences in effectiveness between distance education and face-to-face education.

An Ecosystem: Dancing With Robots and a Transmedia Learning System

As learning differences cannot be unambiguously attributed to any medium of instruction (e.g., radio, TV, computers), we should be advised against a hierarchy paradigm. Instead, we should understand that an effective learning environment consists of a variety of media, as an ecosystem includes all of the living things (e.g., plants, animals, other organisms). This chapter argues that we need to change our perspectives on learning media. These media are not a hierarchy; they are an ecosystem.[1] In an ecosystem, each organism has its own niche and its own role to play. In the same vein, in an optimal learning environment, each learning medium, teachers in particular, should find and occupy its own niche (e.g., the unique functions that this medium has; functions that other media either don't have or cannot perform as well as this particular medium) and complement each other's role in the system.

To view a learning environment as an ecosystem, we have to shift our focus from finding the better (and even the best) learning medium to understanding the niche and the strength of each medium and taking into consideration the interrelationships among these media. To be more precise, we need to first analyze the strengths/niches of computers and humans and then construct a learning environment that taps the strengths/niches of both. This process is illustrated in both *Dancing With Robots* (Levy & Murnane, 2013) and *A Transmedia Learning System for Language Learning* (Zhao, 2011). Levy and Murnane (2013) argue that humans should be "dancing with robots." The main idea is to let computers (i.e., robots) do what they are good at, and humans should be trained to do what computers don't do. Levy and Murnane do a nice job of reviewing "how computers do what they do" and "what computers don't do (yet)" (pp. 6, 9). According to them, computers can substitute for humans when computers have all the needed information to complete the task and such information is reorganized and

---

1. The sentence is inspired by Leonard Cassuto's (2013) article "We're Not a Hierarchy, We're an Ecosystem: Graduate Programs Should Ignore the Ranking and Find Their Niche."

acquired in a form that computers can process. For example, the self-service airport kiosks process information in a "logical, step-by-step procedure":

> Does the name on the credit card match a name in the reservation data base?
>
> If Yes, check for a seat assignment.
>
> If No, instruct customer to see desk agent. (Levy & Murnane, 2013, p. 7)

However, computers cannot perform tasks when they have to solve new problems (i.e., problems that even the "rules writers" did not anticipate) or problems that cannot be processed by prescribed "logical, step-by-step procedures." And that's when human input of cognitive complexity is required. The self-check-in kiosk has to refer customers to a desk agent since the prewritten program doesn't provide alternative reactions when the name on the credit card doesn't match a name in the reservation database. Human work in this example requires skills to communicate (which cannot be programmed since it has to respond to unpredicted responses) and to solve problems in new conditions.

To simultaneously incorporate the strengths of technology and humans and address their limitations, Levy and Murnane (2013) propose a framework of "dancing with the robots." The focus of the framework is to let computers solve routine problems and to direct human work to "solving unstructured problems, working with new information, and carrying out non-routine manual tasks" (p. 3)—three types of tasks that computers cannot successfully perform. In other words, they believe we should use computer competency to complement human skills.

If the current iteration of James Montagnes's question were presented to Levy and Murnane, their answer would be no, teachers cannot be replaced by computers. Instead, they argue that teaching is a profession that requires non-computer skills, such as solving unstructured programs and working with new information. Therefore, teachers won't be simply replaced. "Teaching, selling, managing, reporting—these and many other jobs emphasize communication because their task is to exchange not just information but a particular understanding of information" (Levy & Murnane, 2013, p. 18).

Zhao (2011) illustrates well what a learning ecosystem may look like for language learning. It should include a variety of learning media (including teachers) and it should delegate "different learning activities to the medium that do it the best and involve complete human participation and action" (p. 9). For example, at the stage of practice (see more details in Table 1.1), learners can get practice opportunities from both technology (e.g., online exercises, mobile games) and human resources (e.g., teachers, mentors, peers).

The essence of this new paradigm can be captured by a line from the movie *The Matrix*: "Never send a human to do a machine's job," which is also the title of our book. It shows the significance of first differentiating functions of human beings and technology and then assigning technology or human resources to different activities in the

Table 1.1 Human and Technology Resources for Practice in Language Learning

Computer resources	Human resources (delivered by traditional face-to-face communication and by computer-mediated communication)
Online exercises: These include exercises for basic language mechanics, such as pronunciation, grammar, and vocabulary exercises, that are delivered online. Learners can take online exercises at convenient times and as many times as they want. Learners can also choose exercises that are right at their difficulty level.	**Peer mentors**: Where possible, immigrant children in the same school or a different school (who would speak the first language of language learners) can serve as mentors for language learners. In addition, students with advanced language proficiency can also be mentors.
Mobile games: These include computer games for practices distributed on mobile devices.	**Teachers**: Qualified teachers would provide focused teaching and manage learning activities. **Online language mentors**: Individuals from local communities or elsewhere in the world mentor language learners via computer-mediated communication.

Source: Zhao (2011).

learning process. The ultimate goal is to tap the advantage of both human beings and technology and therefore provide an optimal learning environment for learners.

TECHNOLOGY AND TEACHERS IN A LEARNING ECOSYSTEM: WHAT ARE THEIR NICHES?

When we view a learning environment as an ecosystem, we have to know the niche for each species in the ecosystem (e.g., human teachers, technology; see Table 1.2). The niches for technology are mechanical repetitive tasks, creative ways of presentation and interaction, and opportunities to promote learning.

In contrast, the niches for teachers can be found in critical thinking as well as social and emotional interaction. Here, niches for a species refer to what one species can do and other species either don't do or don't perform equally well or efficiently. For example, for mechanical repetitive tasks (e.g., teaching how to write letters, grading multiple-choice test items), one of the niches for technology, teachers have no problem with completing such tasks. But it would cost an individual teacher significantly more time to complete the same task.

Niches of Technology in Teaching and Learning

Technology is designed to replace or enhance certain functions performed by human beings. As Marshall McLuhan (1964) argues in his

Table 1.2   The Niches of Technology and the Niches for Teachers

Ecosystem components	Niches
Technology	Mechanical repetitive tasks
	Creative ways of presentation and interaction
	Opportunities to promote learning
Teachers	Critical thinking
	Social and emotional interaction

widely read book *Understanding Media*, technology serves as an "extension of man." For example, the bent finger becomes a hook; the human arm and hand become a rake, oar, or shovel; the human nerves become telegraph cables; the lens in the human eye becomes the lens in an optical instrument. Breakthroughs in transportation such as cars and airplanes significantly enhance human beings' ability to travel. As we can see from these examples, technology can do certain things better or with significantly less time, physical effort, or money than human beings can. By the same token, educational technology has its strengths in teaching and learning when compared with teachers.

Mechanical Repetitive Tasks

Although teaching and learning are creative acts, we cannot deny that they also involve rote learning and remembering basic facts. For example, writing the letters of the alphabet is an essential skill for young children. Traditional teaching of letter-writing requires a teacher to provide guides of letter-writing repetitively. Sure, a teacher can demonstrate to the class how to write letters on the board, but to do it repetitively is time-consuming. With games and programs that are designed to teach students letter-writing, teachers can be freed from this mechanical repetitive task.

Letter Writer Oceans is an example of such a program. In this application, the letters float below the ocean's surface. When a learner taps on a letter, the guides for the letter strokes appear. A little fish swims to the beginning of a stroke, where the learner places his or her finger. Then all the learner needs to do is follow the stroke directions and practice writing the letter on the screen. The fish follows the learner's finger as long as he or she is writing correctly.

> The ultimate goal is to tap the advantage of both human beings and technology and therefore provide an optimal learning environment for learners.

Another benefit of computers and other technology is that they make sharing more efficient and less costly. For example, with Google Docs teachers can easily share documents with students. Teachers can define whether their students can only view the document or are allowed to edit it. Teachers can also assign documents to different small groups of students. In addition, Google Docs allows teachers to view student work in the document, provide comments and suggestions, view students' revisions, and resolve any questions or comments that arise. Of course, students can use Google Docs in a similar way for peer reviewing and editing. All of these functions may still be done via email, but you can see that requires more time and a lot more clicks.

Creative Ways of Presentation and Interaction

Developments in educational technology open a plethora of possibilities for presentation and interaction in learning. Technology can infuse more fun into learning by adding multimedia materials that may increase learners' motivation. Letter Writer Oceans, for example, creates a kid-friendly learning environment by using a moving fish as the learning guide for students instead of the traditional lecturing by teachers. In a review by Sivin-Kachala and Bialo (2000), technology was reported to have a positive effect on student attitudes toward learning, self-confidence, and self-esteem. Students who participated in computer-connected learning networks were found to have "increased motivation, a deeper understanding of concepts, and an increased willingness to tackle difficult questions" (Roschelle, Pea, Hoadley, Gordin, & Means, 2000, p. 81). Another review reports effective use of technology led to higher school attendance and lower dropout rates (Coley, 1997).

When technology transforms how materials are presented to learners, it may also help learners remember what is in the materials and therefore lead to better learning outcomes. For example, PowerPoint is widely used in teaching and learning. In fact, it is so widely used that nowadays people expect some kind of multimedia aids in classroom presentations. Multimedia aids such as PowerPoint simultaneously provide students with access to auditory/verbal information (e.g., teachers' lecturing, audio, video) and visual/pictorial information (e.g., illustrations, animation, video, on-screen text). As the cognitive theory of multimedia learning suggests, the human information-processing system contains dual channels (Mayer, 2005). One channel processes auditory/verbal information, and the other processes visual/pictorial information. When multimedia aids are used in learning, students have to process information in both channels, and such deeper processing may lead to better understanding of the presented material.

Personalized Learning Experiences

A typical class includes 20 or more learners with vastly different needs in the classroom. The differences may stem from various levels of academic knowledge and skills, racial and ethnic background, learning styles, and gender. Addressing all of those differences with one uniform curriculum in a constrained time frame can be a daunting task for even an exemplary teacher.

Educational technology tools hold great potential in providing personalized instruction. Compared with human teachers, technology can easily track individual learners' progress and provide immediate feedback to the learners in real time. Based on such data, technology tools can design personalized learning by setting learning objectives at the right difficulty level and creating learning experiences to motivate students.

Tutoring software plays a big role in creating personalized learning experiences. When a learner is working out a series of math problems in tutoring software, the data of that work will be tracked by an advanced personalized learning application. Such data will reveal many of the learner's strengths and weaknesses in solving those math problems. Questions that such data may be able to answer include what types of problems are the most challenging to the learner (which can be indicated by the time that the learner spends on different types of problems) and whether the learner is making consistent mistakes that may suggest his or her misconception. Don't get me wrong, I believe a human teacher can do all of these as well, but human teachers are strongly constrained by time and space. Even the most effective teacher cannot keep an eye on a group of 20 or more learners, looking for any pattern in their mistakes. The recent move to one-to-one computer initiatives, BYOD (bring your own device), and increased access to tablets in schools makes it more possible to provide personalized learning experiences via technology.

Forest Lake Elementary School, in Columbia, South Carolina, successfully used technology to create personalized learning experiences to better serve an increasingly diverse student population. Traditional teaching with a defined lesson targeted to the average-level student can hardly meet the needs of students with different family incomes, ethnicities, family structures, first languages, interests, and academic skills. To support each learner at his or her own level, the Forest Lake teachers and administrative staff employ a variety of digital technology tools (e.g., interactive whiteboards, digital cameras, video cameras, remote-response clickers, PDAs). When asked about designing personalized lessons and creating a positive learning environment, the teachers and staff suggested the final product of students' work can be presented via various technology tools and can be tailored to students' interests and needs (G. Rubenstein, 2010). For example, students working on a project about the Civil War could choose to present their work in a zooming Prezi presentation, a comic strip using Pixton or Comic Life, or a VoiceThread project that invites video, voice, and text commenting. The teachers and staff also suggested delivering instruction through multiple forms of media and using remote-response systems such as clickers to collect and use immediate feedback on individual students' understanding.

Personalized instruction may go beyond the level of individual instructors when it is adopted as a schoolwide instruction model, as evidenced in the School of One (Medina, 2009). The pilot program of the School of One was conducted at Dr. Sun Yat Sen Middle School 131, in New York City's Chinatown. Here, some creative terms are used to mirror the innovative learning model. For example, the learning space arrangements are compared to the traffic patterns at airports, and students' agendas are called playlists. In this program, a student arrives at school in the morning and answers five questions, and his or her answers will be fed into a computer algorithm program to figure out what the learner will be doing that day (i.e., the learner's customized playlist). The algorithm will decide his or her level of learning based on what he or she learned the day before, which teacher the learner will work with today, and even what specific activities he or she will be doing today. A learner's playlist consists of a variety of learning modalities throughout the day: Students may work with computer software individually, in groups, with a virtual tutor, with a live tutor, and so on. The program overthrows the traditional teaching model of one teacher for 25 students in a classroom. Administrators stay in a room and look over more than a dozen computer screens displaying students' playlists and how well learners are navigating them. Joel I. Klein, the New York City schools chancellor, commented that the program learning is innovative since it tailors each lesson to "a student's strengths and weaknesses, as well as the child's interests" (quoted in Medina, 2009, para. 4). The School of One program is expected to be expanded to 50 or more schools in New York.

So we get it. Technology has great potential for learning and can significantly empower learners. Technology is efficient in teaching basic skills repetitively and can therefore save many hours of teaching for human teachers. Thanks to technology, multimedia materials become highly accessible and bring more fun to learning. Last but not least, technology has great potential for providing personalized instruction.

Despite the great potential and affordances of technology, it is dangerous to think that technology is almighty and will completely replace human beings. The takeover may happen for physical labor, but it is not possible in tasks that require critical thinking and social and emotional interaction, which are deemed essential in teaching and learning.

Niches of Teachers in Teaching and Learning

As Levy and Murnane (2013) conclude, the tasks that humans can do more effectively than computers include both high-skilled unstructured tasks and low-skilled tasks. In the context of teaching, these skills and tasks are reflected in critical thinking as well as emotional and social interaction.

Critical Thinking

Teachers are irreplaceable in evaluating educational technology in terms of pedagogy and content. As with other things designed by human beings, technology has flaws and limitations. Educators need to first be mindful of what a particular technology can do (i.e., affordances) and what it may not do so well (i.e., constraints) and then choose appropriate technology tools for learners. This is easier said than done. Education apps and tools experienced explosive growth in recent years. In January 2012, about 1.5 million iPads were used in educational institutions and schools (Rao, 2012). Around the same time, over 500,000 apps were available on iTunes and more than 300,000 for Android (Barseghian, 2012). It was expected that mobile app revenue would continue such dramatic increases and would generate $38 billion by 2015. While it is great news that students may have access to such a great many educational resources, it poses a big question: How do we select the right apps?

This is no easy task. For instance, if an instructor wants to promote communication among students, he or she is blessed with a multitude of technology tools such as wikis, Google Doc, blogs, Twitter, and VoiceThread. These tools, however, promote different types of communication experiences for students due to their particular affordances and constraints. The criteria include but are not limited to whether the tool supports collaborative writing in small groups, whether it offers RSS subscription, whether it limits the length of writing, whether it allows audio comments and feedback, and how that feedback may be shared with others.

The affordances and constraints of these technology tools have to be discussed in the context of teaching. What are the pedagogical and content needs for learners, and how may the technology tool help meet these needs? This issue can be further dissected to include the following questions:

- What content am I teaching with such technology?
- What are the affordances of the technology tool?
- Are there any drawbacks of the technology?
- What are the particular learning needs of my student(s)?
- How am I going to use this technology in my teaching (e.g., teacher use vs. student use; whole-class setting vs. small-group work or individual work; whether to share with people outside the class)?
- How may the use of this technology provide a better learning opportunity for students? Why?

As you see, teachers are engaged in the process of constantly making decisions when they are weighing all the possible ways to use technology. They have to be equipped with appropriate content and pedagogical knowledge to connect their teaching and learning tools and the affordances and constraints of these tools. The Technological Pedagogical Content Knowledge Framework argues that effective technology integration for teaching requires understanding and negotiating the relationships between technology, pedagogy, and content (see Figure 1.1).

Figure 1.1 Technological Pedagogical Content Knowledge (TPACK) Framework

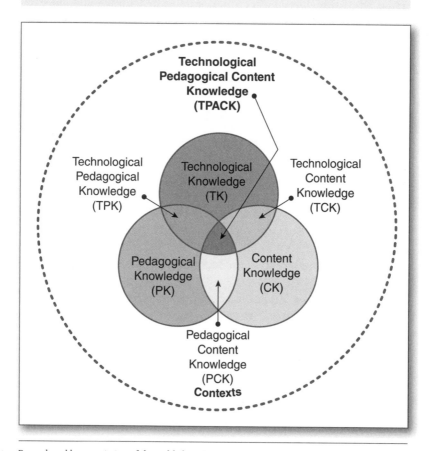

Even for the most experienced teachers, selecting appropriate technology for their particular teaching and learning goals can be a daunting task. First, apps are not described and organized in a consistent way in the iTunes App Store or other app stores. It is hard to discover and explore apps specific to a content area or age group. Second, most user and/or professional reviews of educational apps fail to provide the context in which the app may be used. This context information includes what an app teaches, how lessons are delivered, how the technology may reach students of diverse backgrounds, and how learning with this app may be assessed. Such context information is important and will affect decisions about whether and how to use the technology. Last but not least, oftentimes educational reviewers do not have teaching experience to address essential questions that teachers may have, such as "How may this application work with my students with special needs?" and "Can I provide personalized instruction with this application?" An outsider with little content and pedagogical knowledge may tend to focus on the technical part of the tool and therefore miss the point of always looking at the whole package (i.e., technical, content, and pedagogy).

Teachers have no choice but to review applications themselves. A survey by Harris Interactive found that about one-third of teachers spend an hour or more each week searching for educational technology they can use in their classrooms (Molnar, 2013). But an hour every week is far from enough to get teachers to discover a technology tool with potential for teaching and learning, explore the tool in order to know it well enough to create something that they can use with students, and integrate the technology to better meet students' needs.

In response to the lack of educators reviewing educational technology tools, new websites such as edshelf, Graphite, PowerMyLearning, Edustar, appoLearning, and Learning List have been created to get reviews by educators to help pick best EdTech tools. These sites are sometimes compared with Angie's List or *Consumer Reports*. PowerMyLearning features thousands of free games, videos, and interactives in all major K–12 content areas, and these resources are aligned to the Common Core. For similar objectives, edshelf was created to provide a directory of websites, mobile apps, and desktop programs that are rated and reviewed by parents and educators. Edshelf is now used by teachers in 4,000 school districts. In contrast, AppoLearning takes a more collaborative approach. It invites parents, educators, and other education professionals to review applications and submit their evaluations to the appoLearning Report Card database. Applications are judged on six aspects: educational content, kid appeal, assessment, features and design, value, and safety and privacy. Since these sites have emerged recently, we don't know which may become go-to resources for educators and parents. But the call for more websites with educators' reviews of educational technology illustrates that teachers are essential and irreplaceable, even when we are surrounded by a variety of technology tools.

Social and Emotional Interaction

Teachers are also irreplaceable due to their impact on students' social and emotional development. Teaching and learning mean more than just cognitive development in areas such as being able to read and write, solving math problems, and conducting science experiments. Emotional and social development are two additional essential aspects of development for school-aged children, even though we do not always teach them explicitly. School is a primary setting for children to learn how to make friends; how to maintain friendship; how to interact with adults, including adults with more power (such as teachers); and how to solve problems that emerge in social interaction. Teachers are not replaceable in these areas.

It would be hard to imagine that students could deal with the following social and emotional needs without the social settings provided by schools in general and guidance from teachers in particular.

- how to express their emotions
- how to cope with jealousy
- what to do about concerns related to self-esteem, physical appearance, and academic success
- whether to conform in groups
- how to get acceptance by peers

So the short answer to all versions of James Montagnes's question is no. No, TV will not replace teachers. No, computers will not replace teachers. No, online education will not replace teachers. No, tablets will not replace teachers.

We have been asking the wrong questions. Why do we push ourselves to think which is better, teachers or technology? Why do we intend to choose between the two, teachers or technology? As this chapter has argued, both teachers and technology have unique strengths. With high value in a learning ecosystem, neither technology nor teachers could or should be replaced by the other. If we consider the learning environment as an ecosystem, teachers and technology are two different agencies occupying specific niches, serving different purposes for learners. Teachers have distinct sets of content and pedagogy knowledge, and they can make decisions in complex, dynamic, and unpredictable situations. A teacher in one niche of the learning ecosystem is not "better" than technology, and vice versa. Instead of trying to rank teachers and technology in a hierarchy, we should think of them as important parts of the learning ecosystem. A better question to ask is: How can teachers and technology work together to create a sustainable learning environment.

CONSTRUCTING A LEARNING ECOSYSTEM: WHAT DOES IT LOOK LIKE?

So our (real) job is to create an effective learning environment that taps the strength of technology and teachers. What does it look like? While there is no definite structure of this optimal learning ecosystem, the biggest indicator of success is that the niches of technology and the niches of teachers are incorporated effectively. Technology-powered teachers and flipped classrooms are two examples of learning ecosystems that integrate the strengths of both.

Technology-Powered Teachers

In an effective learning ecosystem, teachers are not replaced by technology. Instead, they are greatly empowered by it and they become "tech-powered teachers," a term Salman Khan (2012) uses in a commentary in *Education Week*. Thanks to the niches of computer technology, tech-powered teachers can better reach students' potentials. As Khan further explains:

> Technology will never replace teachers; in fact, it will make teachers even more important. Technology will give teachers valuable real-time data to diagnose students' weak points and design appropriate interventions. It will enable teachers to more quickly gauge students' comprehension of new topics so they can adjust their lesson plans on the spot. Virtual tools may have the potential to provide educational materials to children who have access to nothing else—say, in a remote village in India—but they will never be a substitute for rich experiences with fellow students and amazing teachers. (para. 8; as first appeared in *Education Week*, October 3, 2012. Reprinted with permission from the author)

Salman Khan's own work of creating and sharing free video tutorials greatly empowers teachers. He is the founder and a faculty member of Khan Academy (www.khanacademy.org), a not-for-profit organization with the mission of providing a free world-class education to anyone, anywhere. Khan Academy has made over 2,000 video tutorials, which cover thousands of topics from basic addition to advanced calculus, physics, chemistry, and biology. More than 1 million unique students use the website every month, and over 30 million lessons have been delivered. Students have access to Khan Academy 24 hours a day, 7 days a week and can select videos according to their own learning needs and pace. Both the anytime, anywhere access and the personalized instruction would be challenging and costly, if not impossible, to be realized by human teachers without technology.

Flipped Classrooms

Another example of combining the strength of technology and teachers to create a better learning environment is flipped classrooms, where students learn lessons at home and do "homework" in class with a teacher's help. One 11th grader at Bullis School, in Potomac, Maryland, had her first experience with a flipped classroom in AP calculus; she learned her lessons at home from videos and other materials that her teacher had made and then would do "homework" problems in class (Strauss, 2012). The student's AP instructor, Stacey Roshan, was introduced to the flipped classroom at a technology conference and realized that this would allow her "to get the lecture out of the class" and provide one-on-one support to students (para. 9). When the student was interviewed, she said she had a successful learning experience with this flipped classroom model. She said she made "faster progress in math this year than ever before" (para. 11). Bullis School is not alone in the success of flipped instruction. Clintondale High School, in Michigan, flipped the entire school curriculum. Many teachers either videotape their lessons themselves or direct their students to Kahn Academy. School administrators said the flipped instruction model has helped bolster the school's attendance rate and that the number of students failing in class has declined (Boss, 2012).

The flipped classroom helps student keep up with lessons. Those who miss class can still have access to the content of that day's lesson. The flipped model uses technology to provide personalized instruction for students in and out of the classroom. Students can view instructional videos and materials at their own pace outside class. These videos can introduce new concepts to students or answer frequently asked questions such as "How do I get to Google Docs?" and "What does APA formatting look like?" Then, instead of answering questions over and over, teachers can record videos on such topics and direct students to a video when they pose a particular question. Students can watch videos or view materials as many times as they need to. They can also pause a video to jot down notes or rewind it to watch the part that they don't yet understand. Personalized instruction is also offered in class when the teacher answers students' questions and provides help to individual learners instead of giving lectures to the whole class in a traditional classroom.

Flipped instruction is a great example of tapping the strengths of teachers and technology. In this example, technology and teachers are not competing with each other. Instead, they supplement each other with their own affordances. Technologies (e.g., videos, presentations) are integrated into the lesson in order to provide students with access to content and instruction. Teachers are still essential in this model since they scaffold individual students' learning and provide help whenever needed. As personnel who know the content, who master a variety of teaching methods to meet students' individual needs, and who can make decisions in dynamic classrooms, teachers are not irreplaceable.

REFERENCES

Allen, I. E., & Seaman, J. (2011). *Going the distance: Online education in the United States, 2011.* San Francisco, CA: Quahog Research Group and Babson Survey Research Group. Retrieved from http://sloanconsortium .org/publications/survey/going_distance_2011

Althaus, S., & Tewksbury, D. (2000). Patterns of Internet and traditional news media use in a networked community. *Political Communication, 17*, 21–45.

Barseghian, T. (2012, January 18). Explosive growth in education apps. *MindShift.* Retrieved from http://ww2.kqed.org

Belson, W. N. (1961). Effects of television on the reading and buying of newspapers and magazines. *Public Opinion Quarterly, 25*, 366–381.

Bernard, R. M., Abrami, P. C., Lou, Y., Borokhovski, E., Wade, A., Wozney, L., Huang, B. (2004). How does distance education compare with classroom instruction? A meta-analysis of the empirical literature. *Review of Educational Research, 74*, 379–439.

Boss, C. (2012, April 9). "Flipped" classes take learning to new place. *Columbus Dispatch.* Retrieved from http://www.dispatch.com

Cavanaugh, C. (2001). The effectiveness of interactive distance education technologies in K–12 learning: A meta-analysis. *International Journal of Educational Telecommunications, 7*(1), 73–78.

Clark, R. E. (1983). Reconsidering research on learning from media. *Review of Educational Research, 53,* 445–459.

Cohen, P., Ebling, B., & Kulik, J. (1981). A meta-analysis of outcome studies of visual based instruction. *Educational Communication and Technology Journal, 29*(1), 26–36.

Coley, L. N. (1997, September). Technology's impact. *Electronic School,* pp. A30–A33.

Digital schools: Can tablets replace teachers? (2013, September 10). *BBC News.* Retrieved from http://www.bbc.com/news/world-europe-2401 5255

Dixon, P., & Judd, W. A. (1977). Comparison of computer-managed instruction and lecture mode for teaching basic statistics. *Journal of Computer Based Instruction, 4*(1), 22–25.

Finholt, T., & Sproull, L. (1990). Electronic groups at work. *Organization Science, 1*(1), 41–64.

Gray, L., Thomas, N., Lewis, L., & Tice, P. (2010). *Teachers' use of educational technology in U.S. public schools: 2009* (NCES 2010-040). Washington, DC: U.S. Department of Education, National Center for Education Statistics. Retrieved from http://nces.ed.gov/pubs2010/2010040.pdf

Hovland, C. I., Lumsdaine, A. A., & Sheffield, F. D. (1949). *Experiments on mass communication.* Princeton, NJ: Princeton University Press.

Kayany, J., & Yelsma, P. (2000). Displacement effects of online media in the socio-economical contexts of households. *Journal of Broadcasting & Electronic Media, 44,* 215–230.

Kaye, B., & Johnson, T. (2003). From here to obscurity? Media substitution theory and traditional media in an on-line world. *Journal of the American Society for Information Science & Technology, 54,* 264–274.

Khan, S. (2012, October 1). The rise of the tech-powered teacher. *Education Week.* Retrieved from http://www.edweek.org

Kulik, C., Kulik, J., & Cohen, P. (1980). Instructional technology and college teaching. *Teaching of Psychology, 7,* 199–205.

Kulik, J., Bangert, R., & Williams, G. (1983). Effects of computer-based teaching on secondary school students. *Journal of Educational Psychology, 75,* 19–26.

Kulik, J., Kulik, C., & Cohen, P. (1979). Research on audio-tutorial instruction: A meta-analysis of comparative studies. *Research in Higher Education, 11,* 321–341.

Lazarsfeld, P. (1940). *Radio and the printed page*. New York, NY: Dell, Sloan & Pearce.

Levy, F., & Murnane, R. (2013). *Dancing with robots: Human skills for computerized work*. Retrieved from http://content.thirdway.org/publications/714/Dancing-With-Robots.pdf

Mayer, R. E. (2005). Cognitive theory of multimedia learning. In R. Mayer (Ed.), *The Cambridge handbook of multimedia learning* (pp. 31–48). New York, NY: Cambridge University Press.

McLuhan, M. (1964). *Understanding media: The extensions of man*. New York, NY: McGraw-Hill.

Medina, J. (2009, July 22). Laptop? Check. Student playlist? Check. Classroom of the future? Check. *New York Times*. Retrieved from http://www.nytimes.com

Mendelsohn, H. (Ed.). (1964). *Listening to radio*. New York, NY: Free Press.

Mitra, S. (2010, September 26). Can computers take the place of teachers? *CNN*. Retrieved from http://www.cnn.com/2010/OPINION/09/26/mitra.technology.learning

Molnar, M. (2013, August 27). New sites aim to help pick best ed-tech tools. *Education Week*. Retrieved from http://www.edweek.org

Montagnes, J. (1954, December 16). Will classroom TV replace teachers? *Eugene Register-Guard*.

Moore, M. (1994). Administrative barriers to adoption of distance education. *American Journal of Distance Education, 8*(3), 1–4.

National Center for Education Evaluation and Regional Assistance. (2007). *Effectiveness of reading and mathematics software products: Findings from the first student cohort*. Retrieved from http://ies.ed.gov/ncee/pdf/20074006.pdf

Oppenheimer, T. (1997, July). The Computer Delusion. *Atlantic Monthly*, p. 1. Retrieved from http://www.theatlantic.com

Quillen, I. (2012, August 7). Quality debated as districts tap tech over teachers. *Education Week*. Retrieved from http://www.edweek.org

Rao, L. (2012, January 19). Apple: 20,000 education iPad apps developed; 1.5 million devices in use at schools. *TechCrunch*. Retrieved from http://techcrunch.com

Roschelle, J. M., Pea, R. D., Hoadley, C. M., Gordin, D. N., & Means, B. M. (2000). Changing how and what children learn in school with computer-based technology. *Children and Computer Technology, 10*(2), 76–101.

Rotherham, A. J. (2012, January 26). Can computers replace teachers? *TIME*. Retrieved from http://ideas.time.com

Rubenstein, E., et al. (1973). *Television and social behavior: Technical report of the Surgeon General's Advisory Committee, Vol. IV*. Washington, DC: U.S. Department of Health, Education and Welfare.

Rubenstein, G. (2010, April 26). Ten tips for personalized learning via technology. *Edutopia*. Retrieved from http://www.edutopia.org

Schramm, W., Lyle, J., & Parker, E. (1961). *Television in the lives of our children*. Stanford, CA: Stanford University Press.

Sivin-Kachala, J., & Bialo, E. (2000). *2000 research report on the effectiveness of technology in schools* (7th ed.). Washington, DC: Software and Information Industry Association.

Sterling, C., & Kittross, J. (1990). *Stay tuned: A concise history of American broadcasting*. Belmont, CA: Wadsworth.

Strauss, V. (2012, June 3). The flip: Turning a classroom upside down. *Washington Post*. Retrieved from http://www.washingtonpost.com

Williams, T. (1986). *The impact of television*. New York, NY: Academic Press.

Zhao, Y. (2011). *A transmedia ecosystem for language learning: A concept paper*. Unpublished manuscript.

CHAPTER TWO

The Wrong Application

Technology as Tools for Consumption
Versus Tools for Creating and Producing

Technology can be used as tools for consumption or as tools for creating and producing. These two approaches are supported by fundamentally different assumptions about how students learn and what their role is in relation to technology. The first approach assumes that students learn mostly by receiving and absorbing existing knowledge, that they are consumers of knowledge, and that technology is there to help them better take in knowledge and improve their academic outcomes. The second approach, on the contrary, views the most critical role of students as creators. Students learn by creating projects and products, forming new knowledge during the process, and communicating and sharing their experiences, feelings, and ideas, often in a collaborative learning context. The role of technology is to empower students in this process.

These two different approaches represent two very different paths that we can take to integrate technology into learning: one in which we use technology to continue what teachers have been doing for centuries (with or without technologies) and one in which we use technology to greatly empower children's learning experiences by helping them create an engaging, rich, and personalized learning environment. Given the increased capacity of technology and easy access to computers and the Internet nowadays, technologies, for better or worse, can be very powerful in either path.

THE FIRST APPROACH: TECHNOLOGY AS A TOOL FOR CONSUMPTION

How we view the human-computer relationship determines how we define our role in this relationship. Our feelings toward technology are mixed and complicated. On the one hand, we love technology and deeply depend on it. It is our love and dependence on technology that drives the continuous and rapid advancement of information technology and that makes us embrace new technology innovations with great enthusiasm. On the other hand, we harbor a deep suspicion and fear of technology, ranging from the fear of being replaced or dominated by it to the fear of being destroyed by it. This fear is most vividly depicted in popular media, from *Metropolis* and *Modern Times,* in which humans are reduced to cogs of the machine, to *Eagle Eye,* in which a computer system skillfully controls people in an attempt to assassinate key members of the government, to the *Matrix* trilogy, in which technology not only controls humans but also consumes them, to *I Legend* and *Wall-E,* in which technology results in near-destruction of human beings and the earth itself.

Both our love and fear of technology embody themselves in the field of education. Our love is demonstrated in the strong advocacy that calls for the use of technology to transform education and to lead us "toward a golden age of American education" (U.S. Department of Education, 2004). This love is also demonstrated in our collective beliefs, as indicated in national educational policies, that technology is not only a tool that addresses challenges in teaching and learning, but also a change agent and a central force in economic competitiveness (Culp, Honey, & Mandinach, 2003).

However, our fear of technology roots much more deeply in everyday practices in schools. Research has found that people are uncertain about what to do with technology and often hold reservations toward the use of it. Parents worry that the use of technology may cause distractions to students (Hu, 2007). Administrators often worry about faculty not prepared to use technology and students being exposed to inappropriate content on the Internet, encountering cyberbullying, or breaching security measures. Teachers fear that computers might reduce their sense of authority and cause them to lose the territory of teaching to disruptive and invasive technology, as suggested in the question "Can technology displace/replace teachers?" Today's information technology makes all human knowledge widely available through ubiquitous access. Therefore, a student can know more about a particular topic by doing research on her own. Thus teachers are expected to shift their role from one of teaching to one of mostly facilitating. This shift may not be welcomed by all teachers.

For example, a new technology trend developed in the last few years, bring your own device (BYOD), sounds not only viable but also necessary as schools face budget cuts and students' ownership of digital devices is increasingly common. However, there is a long way to go before schools embrace this solution. More than half of schools still have a "no personal electronic device allowed at school" policy for students (Project Tomorrow, 2013). Main concerns include liability, teachers being overwhelmed, increased student cheating, or just being afraid of the unknown (Lai, 2012). In a survey conducted for PBS, 14% of respondents believed that "technology is becoming more of a crutch than it ought to be" (VeraQuest, 2013, p. 9).

This fear of technology is one of the driving forces for the first path, which has been the dominant path since the day technology was introduced into classrooms. The beginning of the 21st century marked a significant turn in information technology. Access to the Internet is nearly universal, and highly interactive technology has penetrated nearly every aspect of our daily lives. However, we have been largely continuing the first path, the tradition of treating technology as a tool and students as consumers of knowledge. Furthermore, the current push for standardization and test-based accountability is rushing us further down the first path. According to this path, the priority of using technology in education is to help students meet some standards and get high scores on some standardized tests.

Therefore, unfortunately, at a time when teachers can assign some teaching responsibilities to technology tools and free themselves to exploit their own strengths as communicators, facilitators, and reflectors, technologies are unfortunately often used as tools to simply carry out teachers' current routine practices. At a time when creating, publishing, and sharing is a few clicks away, learners are still often treated as consumers of technology instead of active creators. At a time when technology can provide engaging, collaborative, and personalized learning environments, the great expectations are placed on boosting test scores. Technology can foster more learner-centered learning, but most teachers continue to serve as the authority of knowledge and transfer their knowledge to students.

But the first path and its resulting practices of using educational technologies are defective, and very likely detrimental, in preparing children for the future. The misalignment of technology and human beings in the learning process will continue to prevent us from realizing the full potentials of technology. By viewing technology and teachers as competing agents in providing effective learning environments, the first path fails to see that teachers may be freed from particular teaching responsibilities to focus on tasks that technology cannot achieve by itself, tasks that require higher-order thinking and critical thinking. Viewing technology only as a tool for consumption also fails to help students fully take advantage of available technology and realize their potential. Today's students, often called *digital natives* (Prensky, 2001), are innovative users of available technology and eager adopters of new technology (Rideout, Foehr, & Roberts, 2005). They are not passive consumers of information, but have taken on multiple roles in the digital world, becoming "producers, collaborators, researchers and publishers" (Stead, 2006, p. 6). It is believed that their digital experiences have changed not only the ways they communicate, socialize, and entertain, but also fundamentally how they approach learning (DeDe, 2005; Prensky, 2006). Furthermore, recent neuroscience research has found that extensive experiences involving computers, smartphones, games, and advanced search engines are changing the brain structure and stimulating faster evolution of the brain (Small & Vorgon, 2008).

In addition, using technology as a tool to improve students' academic outcomes, a major goal of investing heavily in educational technology, may not be a realistic goal, as research has repeatedly found that technology has little to no impact on student test scores (Kenny, 2013; Lei & Zhao, 2007; Richtell, 2011).

Gardener and Davis (2013) point out that human beings have been using various tools since the beginning and information-rich technology since the 20th century, yet digital media may represent a "quantum leap" in power and influence (p. 13). It has become apparent that continuing on the first path, in which we treat technology only as tools and students mainly as consumers, cannot help us benefit from the power and influence that today's digital media offers us. Instead, it is time for us to consider an alternative approach, the second path, in which students are viewed as creators, producers, and leaders in the new digital world.

CONSTRUCTIVISM: CONSTRUCTING BY CREATING AND PRODUCING

One major shift in assumptions about education that occurred in the 20th century is that, instead of viewing knowledge as something taught, received, stored, and later retrieved, many researchers believe that knowledge is actively constructed by students through interactions with their physical and social environment and through reorganizing their own mental structures, and students actively construct new knowledge from their experiences in the world—an idea that can be traced back to the theories of Jean Piaget (Bruckman & Resnick, 1995). This constructivism approach calls for students as designers and leaders of technology uses and aims to cultivate learners' autonomy, creativity, and responsibility for their own learning. It also redefines teachers' role in this globalized and digitalized world. Instead of being the authority of knowledge and teaching students something from the never-ending list of technology products, teachers should empower students by encouraging them to discover and pursue their own interests, design and lead their learning by selecting technologies that are appropriate for each learner. To repeat the title of this book, never send a human to do a machine's job. Instead, help a human develop a partnership with a machine and let each work on the part that they are good at.

Modern information and communication technology (ICT) supports constructivist teaching and learning in various ways. First, ICT makes it possible to provide authentic learning settings and processes to students. Students can use technology to solve many daily problems they have: doing homework, searching for information on school work, communicating with friends, developing personal interests, and so on. Wiggins (1993) argues that authentic problems are nonalgorithmic, complex, and amenable to multiple solutions. Therefore, the process of problem solving is a process of thinking that helps students explore the possibilities of different solutions and develop a deep understanding of how they work, so the students can apply similar solutions to solve other problems. In addition, ICT not only helps students find solutions to existing problems, but also changes the problems they have to solve every day. Through this dynamic process, students learn how to solve ever-changing real-world problems and gain an understanding of the affordance and constraints of technology.

Second, ICT provides opportunities for students to construct not only their knowledge, but also actual products. Technology supports learners to construct and represent understanding in tangible forms (e.g., various programming, modeling, and hypothesis testing tools). It engages learners in reflections and discussions to share the knowledge construction process and enhance understanding (e.g., computer-supported collaborative learning). And it enables learners to exercise collaborative problem solving and decision making in learning contexts that simulate realistic contexts (e.g., simulation-epistemic games). Thus, technology defines the participative nature of learning, making education more experience based. As Piaget (2008) points out, "To know an object is to act on it. To know is to modify, to transform the object, and to understand the process of this transformation, and as a consequence to understand the way the object is constructed" (p. 34). Many emerging technologies, including various Web 2.0 tools, make it possible, conducive, and appealing for students to create their own projects and products that can be shared, discussed, examined, and refined.

> Never send a human to do a machine's job. Instead, help a human develop a partnership with a machine and let each work on the part that they are good at.

Third, ICT strengthens the social nature of learning (Brown & Adler, 2008). Technology enables social construction of knowledge through discussions and interactions around problems or actions. Sharing is a critical social component of constructivist learning. Sharing a creation can result not only in its refinement, but also in the learner obtaining a deeper understanding of other people's perspectives on the object and on the ideas related to it (Evard, 1996). With social communication technologies such as blogging, online chatting and discussions, YouTube, Facebook, and wikis, ICT makes it unprecedentedly easy to reach the broadest audience possible. For example, a recent survey of

2,462 Advanced Placement and National Writing Project teachers conducted by the Pew Research Center's Internet & American Life Project found that 96% of the surveyed teachers agreed that digital technologies "allow students to share their work with a wider and more varied audience" and 79% agreed that these tools "encourage greater collaboration among students" (Purcell, Buchanan, & Friedrich, 2013, para. 2). According to the teachers, students' exposure to a broader audience for their work and more feedback from peers encourages "greater investment among students in what they write and greater engagement in the writing process" (Purcell et al., 2013, para. 4).

In addition, technology caters to students' background and empowers them in their constructivist learning process. Modern ICT holds the potential to truly realize the age-old dream of individualized learning—learning that is customizable, catering to individual needs, adjusted to individual abilities, and supporting individual learning styles. Technology makes the field of education increasingly diversified and thus provides more choices to learners, such as different types of learning materials, multiple ways of learning, and various approaches in assessing learning. Therefore, technology enables the creation of learner-generated content, whereby learners generate, select, and appropriate the resources around them to create learning ecosystems that meet their individual learning needs (Luckin, 2010). Technology contributes to this process by giving learners access to a richer collection of resources and serving as the "more abled partner" to facilitate learners' meaning making with the resources around them.

An example of how modern ICT supports constructivist learning is the makerspace movement. Rooted in the technology-driven maker culture that emphasizes learning by doing in a social environment, the makerspace movement is gaining popularity on college campuses as well as in K–12 schools. A makerspace is a physical place where "children, teens, adults and families can tinker, design, and create together. From woodworking and plaster casting to electronics and 3-D printing [the movement] encourages experimentation, open-ended exploration, and believe that making mistakes is a great way to learn" (New York Hall of Science, n.d.). A makerspace is a constructivist environment in every sense: It is a social environment where students work collaboratively on projects, share ideas, and help and learn from each other. It supports hands-on projects and emphasizes the process as well as the product of making. It is an informal learning environment where students can receive advice from experts and their peers. All the projects are authentic and relevant as makers choose what interests them the most to work on; students can work on robotics or making a film. It is a place that inspires curiosity, nurtures creativity, and supports innovation, as students take the ownership of their own project, experimenting with their role as designer, problem solver, and creator. Schools around the globe are making room for makerspaces, and students work on various technology projects, ranging from robotics, filmmaking, and Web programming to 3-D printing, animation, and digital fabrication (Roscorla, 2013). In this case, technology supports constructivist learning in the makerspaces and expands the possibilities that students can explore.

WIKIPEDIA: A MASS PROJECT OF CREATING AND MAKING

In 2012, after 244 years, it was announced that Britannica would no longer print its iconic *Encyclopedia Britannica,* the world's most reputable encyclopedia, a change that many considered the end of an era (Pepitone, 2012). The coming of the end of the printed *Encyclopedia Britannica* is accompanied and mainly caused by the rising of a different type of encyclopedia: free, open, and online. The most influential is Wikipedia, the world's largest online encyclopedia.

There are stark contrasts between the *Encyclopedia Britannica* and Wikipedia:

- number of articles: 65,000 vs. 30 million (ever growing)
- number of languages in which it's available: 1 vs. 287 (so far)
- number of users: thousands or at most a few million vs. 1.2 billion (growing)
- frequency of updates: once in a few decades or several years vs. constantly
- cost of access: thousands of dollars vs. free
- contributors: known experts vs. anyone

Despite these stark contrasts, Wikipedia shares a similar quality that makes *Encyclopedia Britannica* the most reputable encyclopedia:

reliability. A 2005 study published in scientific entries in both Wikipedia and *Encyclo britannica* and found that although the Wikipedia entries were often less well written, there was a similar rate of conceptual errors and factual errors found in entries in both works (Giles, 2005).

With more than 19 million registered user writers around the world, Wikipedia might be the largest online creating and making project ever. Millions of volunteers, the "Wikipedians," not only contribute entries to Wikipedia, but also actively participate in discourse through many Wikipedia channels such as discussion pages, meta-pages, announcement pages, mailing lists, and Internet relay chat. They are active members of the Wikipedia community.

The spirit of Wikipedia is well captured in the words of its founder, Jimmy Wales: "Imagine a world in which every single person on the planet has free access to the sum of all human knowledge" ("Jimmy Wales," n.d.). This spirit was made possible by wiki, a content management system that allows different users to contribute and edit content and thus work collaboratively. It allows users to create, modify, and remove online information at any time and from any location (Rosen & Nelson, 2008). By using specific wiki sites, users are able to easily share information online publicly and to access that information.

Around the world wikis have been used as collaborative tools for groups and individuals in a wide range of classroom settings, such as writing, English language arts methods, Germanic mythology (Lazda-Cazers, 2010; Matthew, Felvegi, & Callaway, 2012; Oatman, 2005), and language learning (Mak & Coniam, 2008). It allows "students to join together in a knowledge-building community" (Jonassen, Howland, Marra, & Crismond, 2008, p. 105) where they can enhance their critical thinking skills (Snodgrass, 2011). One of the distinctive functions of wikis, history and revision records, provides opportunities for users to check their previous work, to compare their work with other members in the group, and to practice negotiation without presence (Hemmi, Bayne, & Land, 2009). With the learning environment formed in the process of communication and negotiation using wikis, researchers suggest that wikis are helpful in developing teachers' knowledge management processes (Biasutti & EL-Deghaidy, 2012).

Wikis can also be very useful when combined with other methods. For example, in a course on knowledge management taught in

Finland, Greece, and Canada, a wiki was used in conjunction with screen capture videos. Students were able to publish their video on the wiki, actively share their knowledge with other students, and learn with other students' uploaded videos (Makkonen, Siakas, & Vaidya, 2011). Oatman (2005) reports how an elementary school teacher in New York used wikis to improve her students' writing skills and to encourage her students to write for the school's Web-based newspaper. Sarah Chanucey, a third-grade teacher, created her own wikis so that her students would have "a communal and fun space" to practice their writing (Oatman, 2005, p. 52). Also, as an assessment tool, wikis are used to foster learner-centered learning (Lazda-Cazers, 2010).

Wikis probably best represent a new trend that Benkler (2006) calls "the rise of effective, large-scale cooperative efforts—peer production of information, knowledge, and culture" (p. 5). These efforts are expanding into many domains, are supported by different platforms, and are widely used for various purposes. Wikipedia Foundations alone has several other projects in addition to Wiki-pedia, such as Wiktionary, Wikibooks, Wikinews, Wikiversity, Wikiquote, Wikimedia Commons, Wikispecies, and Wikivoyage.

User-generated content such as wikis has populated the Internet and is shaping the nature of cyberspace, the direction in which it is going, and the impact online activities have on the real world. In this process, the users are the creators of content, producers of products, active members and leaders of online communities, and energetic entrepreneurs. Take YouTube as an example. A free video-sharing website founded in 2005, YouTube has grown into the third most popular website in the world, with 100 hours of video uploaded every minute and 1 billion unique users every month. With such popularity, YouTube's influence is growing rapidly and permeating the offline world. For example, *Billboard* recently included YouTube streaming data as a factor in the calculation of the Billboard Hot 100 and related genre charts (Billboard Staff, 2013). A *Forbes* article titled "The YouTube Music Awards: Why Artists Should Care" claims that in this digital era, artwork must elicit reactions on YouTube and social media (Thayer, 2013).

Free sharing websites such as YouTube and open-source soft-ware platforms such as wikis and blogging make it unprecedentedly easy for people to find resources on any topic, to share and collabo-rate, to contribute and create, and to make their voice heard in cyberspace and their products viewed and examined by others. These technologies empower users and transform them from being consumers of information into creators of information, participants of online processes, contributors of online communities, and innovators of new projects and products. Technology also provides the platform and the possibility for the innovators to commercialize their products—whether it be a song, a video, an idea, a project, or a type of expertise—and thus turning the users into entrepreneurs.

DIGITAL STORIES, TWITTERS, BLOGS, VIDEOS, AND ROBOTS: NEW GENRES OF CREATING AND MAKING

To express and communicate our thoughts, feelings, and ideas is one of the most basic and fundamental needs that we as human beings rely on for our physical and psychological well-being. The media available at the time determines how we communicate, how many people we can reach, how long our communication records are retained, and how we receive a response. Before any modern technology, including printing, was available, communication was done through verbal and body language, face to face, to a limited amount of people. The invention of printing was a huge leap in communication in terms of the number of people that can be reached across time and distance. The invention of more recent and advanced communication technologies such as radio, telephone, television, and film further significantly diversified the means of communication and the impact of communication.

The Internet has fundamentally changed the nature of communication. In the past, public communication was, in essence, a one-way information flow. At one end were the few learned authorities, or people with the power, expertise, or necessary resources, and at the other end was the general public who received the information. The high cost associated with publishing a manuscript determined that only works that were considered of great value, or written by people with known influence, or after rigorous peer review could be published. Works that did not meet certain standards or whose authors did not have the resources often "perished." In addition, there was little to no interaction between the sender and the receivers of information. For example, readers may have had an opinion about a book, but their opinions did not matter unless they wrote and published a review of this book (and very few of them would). Similarly, the audience of a radio or a TV program may have had suggestions on the topic being discussed, but unless special effort was made, these suggestions would not be heard.

However, in the age of the Internet, communication happens in multiple ways involving multiple parties. Anyone with Internet access can express an opinion, share stories, and make her or his voice heard, and there are so many different ways to do so. Digital storytelling, Twitter, Facebook, and blogs are just a few examples of the increasingly diversified venues of expressing and sharing. And young people, particularly teenagers, are among the most avid users of these new venues. Technologies such as simulation and gaming, virtual communities, the Internet, and multimedia play an increasingly critical role in people's lives through activities such as play, symphony, storytelling, and creating new meanings for our lives.

Digital storytelling has become one new genre of creating and sharing. Storytelling, as pointed out by Daniel Pink (2005), is one of the right-brain-directed thinking aptitudes that we must rely on in the new era. The Internet and multimedia have dramatically transformed this age-old practice. Students can use various media such as text, voice, pictures, videos, hyperlinks, simulations, and cartoons to create a digital story to express their feelings, communicate their ideas, explore a particular topic, or just tell a story. They can share their digital story with their close friends or post it online for millions to see, read, watch, and comment on.

Another new outlet that young people have used in order to create and share is blogs. Through blogging, users share and communicate with others online or keep their personal journals that could gain attention among Web users (Blood, 2002). Blog posts can be shared and hyperlinked to other blogs and websites, while readers are able to post comments on each post (Blood, 2002; Du & Wanger, 2007). Since the official start of blogs in 1997, there have been many content (blog) management tools, such as Blogger, Blogspot, and WordPress to support users in designing and creating their own blogs. Users can also comment and respond to others and customize the layout and plugins to better fulfill their own needs.

Blogs can be useful in all contexts in education settings. In university libraries, blogs can be used for data sharing (Vogel & Goans, 2005). Blogs can be an alternative paperless digital classroom (Du &

Wanger, 2007; Skiba, 2006). They can serve as a tool to enhance writing skills and collaborative learning (Du & Wanger, 2007; Richardson, 2005; Skiba, 2006), to increase social interaction (Dickey, 2004), and to acquire and communicate among teachers and students (Poling, 2005).

For example, let's meet the third graders in Mrs. Yollis's classroom in a suburb of Los Angeles. On their "Meet the Bloggers" page we learn that the 22 kids—11 girls and 11 boys—have many hobbies, yet the one thing they all "absolutely" love is blogging. On the class blog (http://yollisclassblog.blogspot.com), students write about their summer vacations, what books they are reading, and their own stories and adventures. During Family Blogging Month, students involve their family members and relatives in the blogging activities. Their blog has more than 1.6 million visits, and many of them are from outside of the United States, including Europe, Australia, Asia, and Africa! The bloggers even presented at the Texas Google Summit through Google Hangout On Air and shared with the audience their blogging project and what they learn from blogging.

Today's blogging technology is increasingly sophisticated and thus provides an even platform for students to create and share. For instance, Drupal is free and open source software designed as a back-end system for users or communities to create and maintain their websites, including personal blogs, Internet forums, podcasts, photo galleries, and corporate sites. Users are able to publish, organize, and manage information on their sites. In Australia, online astronomy courses at Swinburne University are offered on a website built by Drupal (Barnes et al., 2008). Gaggle, another open source software framework, provides opportunities for K–12 teachers, students, and parents to interact in a safe online environment. In addition to blogging, Gaggle includes many other useful tools such as shared calendar, Dropbox, discussion boards, digital lockers, online document editing, SMS texting, and filtered YouTube access. Robinson High School, in Florida, for example, utilized Gaggle in a digital design class for document editing and collaboration (Akinrefon, 2012).

Students' creation with technology is not limited to the online world. Robots and 3-D printing are just a few examples. The TechEBlog summarized the top 10 student innovations with technology, ranging from a cellphone-controlled tractor to a nuclear reactor ("Top 10 Student Inventions," 2011). For instance, using

Legos and computers, teenagers from New York, Michigan, Illinois, and California created robots that could gather and assemble rocket parts or help humans complete tasks in space, and they competed for a chance to represent the United States in the Robot Olympiad (Lawrence, 2014). Building a robot is a collaborative work involving expertise from different people. It is a complex task, often involving intensive designing, programming, constructing, and experimenting, and this process can go many rounds before the robot is finalized. Each step involves creatively analyzing the task and working on a solution. Around the world, students are creating robots that can be used to solve real problems, such as a robot that can clean solar panels (Singh, 2014) or a robotic hand to help an 8-year-old boy play sports (Boccella, 2014). Similarly, other student technology inventions have real impact in life. For example, four students from Portland State University worked collaboratively to build a computer-aided pill identifier. This invention not only can save lives, but also helped its creators win at the Cornell Cup USA national design competition in 2012 (Budnick, 2012).

DIVERSE NEEDS AS CREATORS AND MAKERS

John Dewey suggested that there are four categories of natural impulses: to inquire or to find out things, to use language and thereby to enter into the social world, to build or make things, and to express one's feelings and ideas. Based on his ideas, Bruce and Levin (1997) proposed a taxonomy of technology that identified four main functions built on the natural impulses to learn and grow: technology as media for inquiry, for communication, for construction, and for expression. They also outline specific ways in which technology enables students to inquire, communicate, construct, and express. Today this taxonomy still makes good sense, and the only difference is probably that today's technology provides even greater possibilities in each of these aspects and thus enables students to take on multiple roles as creators, producers, leaders, and entrepreneurs.

> For students to be able to actively and creatively participate in the digital world, their diverse needs as creators and makers must be met.

We all are born with the potential to innovate and create, but most of us need a lot of practice in the appropriate context to get really good with it. For students to be able to actively and creatively participate in the digital world, their diverse needs as creators and makers must be met.

First, needless to say, access is the most basic aspect of digital participation. While access to technology in schools has greatly increased, ironically, technology itself has become one area where inequity lies. The gap between students who have access to technology and those who do not is increasing. Affluent parents and children have regular access to Internet resources, digital reference resources, and the tools of digital commerce and interaction, while students from disadvantaged backgrounds have only limited access to technology and to digital resources. According to the 2013 survey of AP and National Writing Project teachers mentioned earlier, 84% of teachers surveyed said that digital technologies are leading to greater disparities across schools (Purcell et al., 2013). Only 54% of the teachers said all or almost all of their students have sufficient access to digital tools while in school, and only 28% said that, at home, only some or hardly any of the students have sufficient access to the Internet and other digital tools they need to effectively complete school assignments. The issue of the digital divide must be addressed, as students from disadvantaged backgrounds not only are denied the routine benefits of technology, they often fail to appreciate technology because of unfamiliarity or lack of exposure.

Second, it is important to provide students with a wide array of technological options to explore what is possible for them. Today's technology provides immense opportunities for students to inquire, communicate, construct, and express. Even for the same purpose, there are various technology tools and contexts that teachers and students can choose from. For example, in order to increase interactions after class with their students, teachers at Odyssey Charter High School explored different social networking options. They first tried Facebook groups and found that the students engaged in quality discussions. However, due to safety concerns about Facebook's requirement to have an individual profile page in order to join a group, they had to drop Facebook groups as the social networking tool. Instead, a Ning network allowed teachers and students to communicate in a more casual way than often occurred via other media.

It also provided support for students' learning activities in a variety of classes, allowing students to create webpages for projects or participate in online discussions with other students (Barbour & Plough, 2009). In another high school with a low-income student population, students used social networking sites for learning 21st century skills. Students believed they gained technical skills through their use of MySpace, primarily learning them in informal settings independently or from friends. Some students showed evidence of expanding on technical skills learned in school (such as video editing) through inclusion of content and features on their MySpace pages (Greenhow & Robelia, 2009).

Third, in order for students and teachers to reap the benefits of the vast resources and opportunities today's technology offers, schools must find a better way to balance the need for security and the need to provide the best learning opportunities for students. Too many schools have invested huge amounts of money in buying advanced technology devices for their teachers and students in the hope of transformed learning, yet at the same time blocking a significant number of resources because of concerns over safety. While filtering and blocking may not be able to effectively protect students from cyber harms, they do effectively block opportunities for students to better inquire, communicate, construct, and express. For example, one of the most famous and influential educational websites, Khan Academy, which offers thousands of tutorial videos on over 100,000 topics, hosts all its videos on YouTube—a website commonly blocked by schools.

Fourth, teachers must build a healthy relationship with technology so that technology empowers them, complements what they can do the best, and works with them to create the best learning experiences for students. It is important to recognize that technology and teachers are both important enablers of learning (Luckin, 2010), and determining the role of each in the education process depends on a critical analysis of their respective strengths in specific learning tasks. For example, technology has some advantages, including providing motivating means for students to learn, operating in environments where humans cannot, providing a great range of resources, enhancing student voice and autonomy in the learning process, and supporting differentiated learning. However, technology is weak in supporting the social aspects of learning such as collaboration and interaction among students and teachers, value acquisition, and thinking development (Salomon, 2001). Even when an instructional step is predominantly mediated by technology, teachers still play a critical role in streamlining, scaffolding, and maximizing the learning experience (Kim & Hannafin, 2011). Therefore, balancing the role of technology and teachers in the education process is essential to the reasonable appropriation of resources for learning and to the maximization of the potential of technology for learning.

Finally, students must develop a healthy relationship with technology. Schools need to provide career and technology education programs that enable students to become inventors and innovators with the use of technology. Students may start from identifying a problem or a specific idea, then compare possible solutions, locate resources, work on a technological product, and even advertise and sell the product online. Through processes like this, students become creative and resourceful problem solvers and may go on to become entrepreneurs.

Today's students live in an era that is both exciting and challenging in unprecedented ways. It is essential for new generations of citizens to be well prepared to participate in the digital era competently and successfully. The virtual world differs from the traditional physical world in fundamental ways, including the tools required for participation, the rules that govern activities, and the consequences of participation, but the multimedia nature of these tools requires different skills than traditional verbal abilities. Competent citizens of the 21st-century world need a sound understanding of the nature of the virtual world, a positive attitude about its complexities, and the ability to create digital products and services in order to participate in and lead its activities. We will address this issue in greater detail in Chapter 4.

REFERENCES

Akinrefon, T. (2012). Gaggle: The safe LMS. *Distance Learning, 9*(3), 21.

Barbour, M., & Plough, C. (2009). Social networking in cyberschooling: Helping to make online learning less isolating. *TechTrends, 53*(4), 56–60.

Barnes, D. G., Fluke, C. J., Jones, N. T., Maddison, S. T., Kilborn, V. A., & Bailes, M. (2008). Swinburne astronomy online: Migrating from "PowerPoint" on CD to a Web 2.0 compliant delivery infrastructure. *Australasian Journal of Educational Technology, 24,* 505–520.

Benkler, Y. (2006). *The wealth of networks: How social production transforms markets and freedom*. New Haven, CT: Yale University Press.

Biasutti, M., & EL-Deghaidy, H. (2012). Using Wiki in Teacher Education: Impact on Knowledge Management Processes and Student Satisfaction. *Computers & Education, 59,* 861–872.

Billboard staff. (2013). Hot 100 news: Billboard and Nielsen add YouTube video streaming to platforms. *Billboard.* Retrieved from http://www.billboard.com/articles/news/1549399/hot-100-news-billboard-and-nielsen-add-youtube-video-streaming-to-platforms

Blood, R. (2002). *The weblog handbook: Practical advice on creating and maintaining your blog.* Cambridge, MA: Perseus.

Boccella, K. (2014). Westtown students create robotic hand for 8-year-old. *Philly.com.* Retrieved from http://articles.philly.com

Brown, J. S., & Adler, R. P. (2008). Minds on fire: Open education, the long tail, and learning 2.0. *EDUCAUSE Review, 43*(1), 17–32.

Bruce, B., & Levin, J. A. (1997). Educational technology: Media for inquiry, communication, construction, and expression. *Journal of Educational Computing Research, 17*(1), 79–102.

Bruckman, A., & Resnick, M. (1995). The MediaMOO Project: Constructionism and professional community. *Convergence, 1*(1), 94–109.

Budnick, N. (2012, May 17). Portland State University students' invention tops the field at national engineering competition. *The Oregonian.* Retrieved from http://www.oregonlive.com

Culp, K. M., Honey, M., & Mandinach, E. (2003). *A retrospective on twenty years of education technology policy.* Washington, DC: U.S. Department of Education, Office of Educational Technology. Retrieved from http://www.ed.gov/rschstat/eval/tech/20years.pdf

DeDe, C. (2005, January 1). Planning for neomillennial learning styles. *Educause Review.* Retrieved from http://www.educause.edu

Dickey, M. (2004). The impact of web-logs (blogs) on student perceptions of isolation and alienation in a web-based distance-learning environment. *Open Learning, 19,* 279–291.

Du, H., & Wanger, C. (2007). Learning with weblogs: Enhancing cognitive and social knowledge construction. *IEEE Transactions on Professional Communication, 50*(1), 1–16.

Evard, M. (1996). A community of designers: Learning through exchanging questions and answers. In K. Kafai & M. Resnick (Eds.), *Constructionism in practice: Designing, thinking and learning in a digital world* (pp. 223–240). Mahwah, NJ: Lawrence Erlbaum.

Gardener, H., & Davis, K. (2013). *The app generation: How today's youth navigate identity, intimacy, and imagination in a digital world.* New Haven, CT: Yale University Press.

Giles, J. (2005). Internet encyclopedias go head to head. *Nature, 438,* 900–901.

Greenhow, C., & Robelia, B. (2009). Informal learning and identity formation in online social networks. *Learning, Media & Technology, 34*(2), 119–140.

Hemmi, A., Bayne, S., & Land, R. (2009). The appropriation and repurposing of social technologies in higher education. *Journal of Computer Assisted Learning, 25*(1), 19–30.

Hu, W. (2007, May 4). Seeing no progress, some schools drop laptops. *New York Times.* Retrieved from http://www.nytimes.com

Jimmy Wales. (n.d.). *Wikiquote.* Retrieved from http://en.wikiquote.org/wiki/Jimmy_Wales

Jonassen, D., Howland, J., Marra, R. M., & Crismond, D. (2008). *Meaningful learning with technology* (3rd ed.). Upper Saddle River, NJ: Pearson/Merrill Prentice Hall.

Kenny, C. (2013, November 11). The false promise of classroom technology. *Business Week.* Retrieved from http://www.businessweek.com

Kim, M. C., & Hannafin, M. J. (2011). Scaffolding 6th graders' problem solving in technology-enhanced science classrooms: A qualitative case study. *Instructional Science, 39,* 255–282.

Lai, E. (2012, July 16). Infographic: The ten things we fear (and love) about BYOD. *Forbes BrandVoice.* Retrieved from http://www.forbes.com

Lawrence, E. D. (2014, September 27). Students hope to represent U.S. in Robot Olympiad. *USA Today.* Retrieved from http://www.usatoday.com

Lazda-Cazers, R. (2010). A course wiki: Challenges in facilitating and assessing student-generated learning content for the humanities classroom. *Journal of General Education, 59*(4), 193–222.

Lei, J., & Zhao, Y. (2007). Computer uses and student achievement: A longitudinal study. *Computers & Education, 49,* 284–296.

Luckin, R. (2010). *Re-designing learning contexts: Technology-rich, learner-centered ecologies.* Abingdon, UK: Routledge.

Mak, B., & Coniam, D. (2008). Using wikis to enhance and develop writing skills among secondary school students in Hong Kong. *System, 36,* 437–455.

Makkonen, P., Siakas, K., & Vaidya, S. (2011). Teaching knowledge management by combining wikis and screen capture videos. *Campus-Wide Information Systems, 28,* 360–366.

Matthew, K. I., Felvegi, E., & Callaway, R. A. (2012). Wiki as a collaborative learning tool in a language arts methods class. *Australian Educational Computing, 27*(1), 39–47.

New York Hall of Science. (n.d.). *Maker Space @ NYSCI.* Retrieved from http://makerspace.nysci.org

Oatman, E. (2005). Make way for wikis. *School Library Journal, 51*(11), 52–54.

Pepitone, J. (2012, March 24). Encyclopedia Britannica to stop printing books. *CNN.* Retrieved from http://money.cnn.com

Piaget, J. (2008). Development and learning. In M. Gauvain & M. Cole (Eds.), *Readings on the development of children* (5th ed., pp. 33–41). New York, NY: Worth.

Pink, D. H. (2005). *A whole new mind: Moving from the information age to the conceptual age.* New York, NY: Penguin.

Poling, C. (2005). Blog on: Building communication and collaboration among staff and students. *Learning and Leading with Technology, 32*(6), 12–15.

Prensky, M. (2001). Digital natives, digital immigrants. *On the Horizon, 9*(5), 1–6.

Prensky, M. (2006). Listen to the natives. *Educational Leadership, 63*(4), 8–13.

Project Tomorrow. (2013). *From chalkboards to tablets: The emergence of the K–12 digital learner.* Retrieved from http://www.tomorrow.org/speakup/SU12_DigitalLearners_StudentsTEXT.html

Purcell, K., Buchanan, J., & Friedrich, L. (2013). *The impact of digital tools on student writing and how writing is taught in schools.* Retrieved from http://www.pewinternet.org/2013/07/16/the-impact-of-digital-tools-on-student-writing-and-how-writing-is-taught-in-schools

Richardson, W. (2005). New Jersey high school learns the ABCs of blogging. *T.H.E. Journal, 32*(11), 40.

Richtell, M. (2011, September 3). In classroom of future, stagnant scores. *New York Times.* Retrieved from http://www.nytimes.com

Rideout, V. J., Foehr, U. G., & Roberts, D. F. (2005). *Generation M: Media in the lives of 8- to 18-year-olds.* Washington, DC: Kaiser Family Foundation. Retrieved from http://kff.org/other/event/generation-m2-media-in-the-lives-of

Roscorla, T. (2013). *Why the "maker movement" is popular in schools.* Retrieved from http://www.centerdigitaled.com/news/Maker-Movement-Popular-Schools.html

Rosen, D., & Nelson, C. (2008). Web 2.0: A new generation of learners and education. *Computers in the Schools, 25,* 211–225.

Salomon, G. (2001). *Technology and education in the age of information.* Haifa, Israel: Zmora-Bitan.

Singh, T. (2014). *Students create award-winning robot that cleans solar panels.* Retrieved from http://inhabitat.com/students-create-award-winning-robot-that-cleans-solar-panels

Skiba, D. (2006). Web 2.0: Next great thing or just marketing hype? *Nursing Education Perspectives, 27,* 212–214.

Small, G., & Vorgon, G. (2008). *iBrain: Surviving the technological alteration of the modern mind*. New York, NY: Riverhead.

Snodgrass, S. (2011). Wiki Activities in blended learning for health professional students: Enhancing critical thinking and clinical reasoning skills. *Australasian Journal of Educational Technology, 27*, 563–580.

Stead, G. (2006). Mobile technologies: Transforming the future of learning. In A. Pinter (Ed.), *Emerging technologies for learning* (pp. 6–15). Coventry, UK: British Educational Communications and Technology Agency.

Thayer, K. (2013). The YouTube Music Awards: Why Artists Should Care. *Forbes*. October 29, 2013. http://www.forbes.com/sites/katheryn thayer/2013/10/29/the-youtube-music-awards-why-artists-should-care/

Top 10 student inventions. (2011). *TechEBlog*. Retrieved from http://www.techeblog.com/index.php/tech-gadget/top-10-student-inventions

U.S. Department of Education. (2004). *Toward a new golden age in American education: How the Internet, the law and today's students are revolutionizing expectations*. Washington, DC: Author.

VeraQuest. (2013). *Teacher technology use*. Retrieved from http://www.scribd.com/doc/123797788/Teacher-Technology-Usage-2013

Vogel, T., & Goans, D. (2005). Delivering the news with blogs: The Georgia State University library experience. *Internet Reference Services Quarterly, 10*(1), 5–27.

Wiggins, G. P. (1993). *Assessing student performance*. San Francisco, CA: Jossey-Bass.

CHAPTER THREE

The Wrong Expectation

Technology to Raise Test Scores Versus
Technology to Provide Better Education

It is tempting, if the only tool you have is a hammer, to treat everything as if it were a nail.

—Abraham Maslow (1966, pp. 15–16)

What Maslow didn't say but also holds a great deal of truth is if you think nails are your only problem, everything looks like a hammer. That's what has been going on in the field of education in the United States. In the last three decades, it has been widely reported that the academic achievement of school-aged children in the United States is low. The commonly used indicators of the low academic achievement of U.S. students are international benchmarks such as the Program for International Student Assessment (PISA) and Trends in International Mathematics and Science Study (TIMSS). In PISA 2012, the United States ranked 26th in math, 21st in science, and 17th in reading; in TIMSS 2011, it ranked 15th in fourth-grade math and 24th in eighth-grade math (National Center for Education Statistics, 2011). Low test scores are identified as the crux of the problem of U.S. education, or to use Abraham Maslow's term, the "nails."

As a result, finding a "hammer" to boost test scores is perceived by many as a fine goal in education. The search for a hammer occurs everywhere in the field of education. Various types of schools (e.g., public schools, private schools, charter schools, online schools, schools from another country), personnel (e.g., teachers, administrators, coaches), and resources (e.g., professional development, technology) are approached as the potential hammers.

This hammer-seeking scheme radically distorted the use of technology in teaching and learning. Technology is expected by many to address the seemingly pressing need of improving test scores. Can this technology improve test scores? Will this technology increase students' performance on international benchmarks? Such expectations mistakenly equate education to test grades. This intolerably narrow definition of education should be corrected. Technology should be put to better uses than improving test scores. The better uses include but are not limited to digital textbooks, personal learning networks, collaboration, personalized learning experiences, and more power for students.

CAN TECHNOLOGY BOOST TEST SCORES? DON'T LET THE WRONG QUESTION GUIDE OUR TECHNOLOGY USE

The value of technology has been questioned repeatedly. The doubt and disappointment directed at educational technology largely stem from the lack of evidence that technology can significantly boost test scores. For instance, a *New York Times* article questioned whether investments in educational technology were worth it (Richtel, 2011). As reported in this article, the Kyrene School District, an innovator in technology integration in Arizona, was challenged about its technology budget as its reading and math scores stagnated, even as statewide scores have risen. Kyrene serves 18,000 K–8 students, mostly from the cities of Tempe, Phoenix, and Chandler, and has been recognized as an exemplary school district for technology integration by the National School Boards Association and has earned widespread praise. In 2008 the National School Boards Association arranged a visit by 100 educators from 17 states to see how Kyrene had made successful innovation by integrating technology in its curriculum. In the technology-centric classrooms, "students are bent over laptops, some blogging or building Facebook pages from the perspective of Shakespeare's characters" (para. 2). "Classrooms are decked out with laptops, big interactive screens and software that drills students on every basic subject" (para. 3). Unfortunately, none of these seemed to be considered as valid indicators of academic performance when compared with test scores. When the test scores in Kyrene came back as flat and disappointing, the district went back to local voters for approval of $46.3 million more in taxes over 7 years for educational technology investment.

Kyrene was just one of the thousands of schools that had to confront doubts about educational technology when test scores were not in their favor. Some school districts have abandoned one-to-one laptop programs since those programs showed "little, if any, measurable effect on grades and test scores" (Hu, 2007, para. 7). The districts and programs that have given up on laptops include all kinds of programs—large and small school districts, urban and rural schools, and schools in high and low socioeconomic areas. Here are a few examples (Hu, 2007):

- The Liverpool High School, just outside Syracuse, New York, decided to phase out laptops. "After seven years, there was literally no evidence it had any impact on student achievement—none," said Mr. Lawson, the school board president in Liverpool (para. 5).
- Matoaca High School eliminated its 5-year laptop program when its students showed no academic gains compared with counterparts without laptops.
- Everett A. Rea Elementary School, in Costa Mesa, California, along with another school, eliminated its use of laptops. Both schools were part of a study of 10 schools in California and Maine from 2003 to 2005, which showed no evidence to support that laptops could increase state test scores.

At the same time, wishful thoughts of technology are easily found in news headlines: "Want Increased Student Achievement Using iPads?" (Norris & Soloway, 2012), "Mobile Apps and Devices Increase Student Achievement" (Tomaszewski, 2012), and "Realizing Increased Student Achievement With Mobile Technologies: Here's the Plan" (Soloway & Norris, 2013).

While there is nothing wrong with wishing that technology would result in higher test scores and better student performance, it is very dangerous to put all of our attention on test scores and allow testing to guide our decisions regarding technology use. We have to examine the testing fever—Why can we not help but get anxious about test scores? What is the historical and cultural context of testing fever? What caused our anxiety about testing scores to get unprecedentedly high at the turn of the 21st century? Could this testing fever be a false alarm?

This ill-defined technology use (and learning at a broader level) is driven by a testing fever that is well represented in No Child Left Behind and Race to the Top. Now the stakes of tests get so high that they play a pivotal role in so many, if not all, aspects of schooling, such as school funding, teacher evaluation, and student recruitment, just to name a few. In other words, the outcomes of students' performance are greatly factored into the future and work life of teachers and administrators. Students need good scores to move up to the next grade, to be admitted to the school/program/university they applied to, and to graduate with a glorious transcript. Teachers need students' good test performance to get merit pay and in some cases to keep their jobs. Administrators need students' high scores to retain school funding and to attract qualified teachers.

In such a fierce and rigid environment that seeks high test scores, it seems almost natural to think about how to use technology for this purpose. But focusing technology uses on improving test scores is wrong, and the urgency of meeting external standards doesn't make it less wrong. Here are the reasons.

First, high test scores don't mean high cognitive skills. Standardized tests are often associated with cognitive abilities. However, higher test scores don't guarantee higher cognitive abilities. Cognitive abilities include *crystallized intelligence* and *fluid intelligence* (Cattell, 1971). Crystallized intelligence is reflected in the knowledge and skills that students acquire in school, and high-stakes tests are designed to measure crystallized intelligence. Fluid intelligence, on the other hand, is the ability to analyze abstract problems and think logically. Even when test scores go up, fluid intelligence doesn't necessarily get higher, as found in a recent study by Massachusetts Institute of Technology neuroscientists and education researchers at Harvard University and Brown University (Massachusetts Institute of Technology, 2013). This study of 14,000 eighth graders in Boston schools found that some schools that had successfully raised students' scores on the Massachusetts Comprehensive Assessment System had almost no effect on students' performance on tests of fluid intelligence skills, such as working memory capacity, speed of information processing, and ability to solve abstract problems.

Second, by using technology to pursue high test scores, we are overlooking nonacademic skills that are big factors in student learning. Noncognitive traits and behaviors may be as important as—or even more important than—cognitive skills in determining academic performance and employment outcomes (Heckman, Stixrud, & Urzua, 2006). In a comprehensive review of nonacademic skills and traits that are associated with influencing academic outcomes for K–12 students, Rosen, Glennie, Dalton, Lennon, and Bozick (2010) identified seven factors: motivation, effort, self-regulated learning, self-efficacy, academic self-concept, antisocial and prosocial behavior, and coping and resilience. Their comprehensive review presents mounting evidence that these factors play a critical role. For example, first-grade teacher ratings of children's temperament and disposition are positively associated with years of schooling at age 22 (Entwisle, Alexander, & Olson, 2005). In addition, poor behavior in eighth grade is negatively related with future educational attainment (Segal, 2008).

> High test scores don't mean high cognitive skills.

Third, high-stakes testing has inherent drawbacks—testing burnout and teaching to the test—and it is almost impossible to fix these problems.

Too Much Testing

Testing and test preparation take a great amount of instruction time and money. The American Federation of Teachers recently studied schools' standardized testing calendars (Nelson, 2013). Two medium-sized U.S. school districts participated in the study, one in the Midwest and one in the East. The total number of test administrations reached 34 in one school district. The other school district had 12 different standardized assessments but 47 separate test administrations in one year. The report concluded:

> If testing were abandoned altogether, Midwestern School District could add from 20 to 40 minutes of instruction to each school day of most grades. In grades 6–11, Eastern School District could add almost an entire class period each day. (p. 26)

In addition, testing accounts for a significant amount of each school district's budget. The Midwestern district spent $600 or more for standardized testing per student in Grades 3–8. The bill was even higher for the Eastern district, more than $1,100 on testing per student in Grades 6–11 every year, $700–$800 per student for Grades 3–5, and about $400 per student in Grades 1–2.

Teaching to the Test

One of the unavoidable side effects of high-stakes testing is more and more teaching to the test. Ron Berler (2013), a journalist who has written for the *New York Times* and *Chicago Tribune*, spent a year at Brookside Elementary School, in Norwalk, Connecticut, and documented his observation in his book *Raising the Curve: A Year Inside One of America's 45,000 Failing Public Schools*. Brookside was one of 45,000 failing public schools during the 2010–2011 school year. What struck Berler was the effect of excessive testing on elementary school curriculum. It was reported that during the fall semester Brookside was like any school you would imagine. But when students returned from Christmas break, for the next 9 weeks until testing began, the school became a test-prep monster. What it did was drop its curriculum, drop its texts, and instead have students study exclusively from a standardized test prep book. Kids were getting a narrow language and math curriculum, nothing close to a liberal arts education. In addition, instruction time and resources were distributed unequally among students for a better chance in getting students to pass standardized tests. In particular, for 22% of the school year, teachers taught primarily to the broad middle section of kids that were going to pass. The school also reached out to those students thought to be on the edge of possibly passing. As a result, the top kids and the bottom kids were left out since instruction for them would not improve the school's testing performance.

PROVIDING BETTER EDUCATION: THE REAL VALUE OF EDUCATIONAL TECHNOLOGY

Test grades are not the gold standard and should not guide our technology use. So what should then? Karen Cator, director of the Office

of Educational Technology in the U.S. Department of E
standardized test scores were an inadequate measure
technology in schools. Ms. Cator, a former executive ...
Computer, was more optimistic about flat scores in a technology-rich
learning environment. "In places where we've had a large implementing of technology and scores are flat, I see that as great," she said
(quoted in Richtel, 2011, para. 44). She also stressed that "test scores
are the same, but look at all the other things students are doing: learning to use the Internet to research, learning to organize their work,
learning to use professional writing tools, learning to collaborate with
others" (para. 44). These are things we don't count if we mindlessly
narrow the value of education to a few numbers on report cards. But
these are things that really matter if we believe that students are owners of their learning and that learning should lead them to solving
real-world problems instead of getting a decent score on a standardized test. As Mark Share, director of technology in the Kyrene School
District, in Arizona, says in the signature file at the bottom of every
email he sends: "It's not the stuff that counts—it's what you do with it
that matters" (para. 45). There are four profound changes that technology has brought into teaching and learning: digital textbooks, personal learning networks, collaboration, and the iLearn model.

Digital Textbooks

Textbooks, which have played an essential role in learning for
centuries, are undergoing significant changes. As more and more
university and schools adopt 1:1 initiatives, they are transitioning
from traditional textbooks to digital textbooks. University of
Massachusetts Boston launched an iPads in the Classroom program
in 2012. In this program, iPads were installed in classrooms for pro-
fessors and students to use during lectures and for interactive activities. Mary Simone, who directs the iPads in the Classroom initiative
in the university, emphasized that iPads have significantly enhanced
the university's learning environment:

> A music theory class gets to play with a piano keyboard app
> to practice keys and harmony. . . . And a physics professor
> can use various astronomy apps to pinch and zoom around
> the night sky, focusing on individual stars, as well as seeing
> statistics on those stars. (quoted in Louie, 2013, para. 2)

The movement toward digital textbooks is also widely seen in K–12 schools. Archbishop Stepinac High School, in White Plains, New York, for example, made nearly every textbook—from freshman biology to senior calculus—accessible on students' laptops and tablets (Fitzgerald, 2013).

Compared with traditional textbooks, digital textbooks have several new features. First, digital textbooks change the way students get knowledge. Students can download all the lesson materials, which means students have access to digital textbooks whenever they have a device (e.g., computer, tablet, mobile phone) and access to the Internet.

Second, in addition to the text found in traditional physical textbooks, digital textbooks also include multimedia materials (e.g., videos, simulations, PowerPoint slides, interactive activities), which have no place in traditional textbooks. A digital textbook allows learners to move objects around on the page, view a digital storytelling of their favorite book, or take an impromptu biology quiz. Textbooks are no longer just reading materials. By providing learning materials, engaging learning activities, and even feedback and assessment, digital textbooks greatly expand on the power of traditional paper-based textbooks and can assume a great many responsibilities in learning.

Third, with authoring tools such as iTunes U Course Manager, teachers are empowered to create their own digital textbooks or a "course packet," which may better accommodate the needs of their students. Teachers can choose content that is developmentally appropriate for their students, include materials and activities that are culturally responsive to their students, incorporate teacher-made videos, and organize the textbook to coordinate with their class schedules.

But none of this comes to teachers easily. It requires three steps—aggregation, curation, creation—and each step involves technology use. First, you need to gather all your sources of information. The best way might be aggregating content through online social bookmarking tools such as Diigo, which allow you to bookmark, tag, annotate, and share sites. You can also connect with other teachers with similar interests and look over resources they have found and shared. The second step is curation. At this step, you need to conduct a deeper analysis of sites you have stored and select sources with the most relevant information for your course/topic. You may want to try LiveBinders, which makes it very easy to post resources for your course, or Scoop-it!, which enables you to create your own online magazine. The last step is creation. That's when you create and publish your digital textbook. Digital tools such as Google Sites, PBworks, Wikispaces, and iTunes U are good choices. With these tools you can publish text, post images, embed videos and multimedia presentations, and include assessment.

Personal Learning Networks

As social media are widely used for connection and collaboration, resources are not isolated from each other. Instead, resources are connected with each other if they are related in some way, maybe via sharing the topic, sharing the interest, or being published or saved. Such connection makes it possible and also important for teachers to create and maintain a personal/professional learning network (PLN). PLNs can significantly help educators grow professionally. Each PLN is created and personalized based on professional interests and goals. Twitter and Pinterest are two examples of social media that can be used for PLNs.

Twitter

Twitter is a social networking and microblogging tool that allows users to send out short messages called *tweets*. Tweets are limited to 140 characters, which makes them easy to skim. Twitter is used by people in many countries around the world, which means teachers have access to thousands of teachers around the world who can contribute to each other's professional growth. There are several ways to use Twitter to create and expand a PLN. First, you can search within the database of Twitter users to find those whose tweets interest you. By following those teachers, you will get updates from them. Chances are their new tweets are about education and will interest you. You can also use hashtags to stay connected with your PLN. When people tweet, they flag their tweet with hashtags (using #, which used to be known as the pound key). Hashtags group information by subject and make it easier to search for and access later. For example, if you are excited about educational technology, you may want to search for the hashtag #edtech. It is important that you not only find information marked with hashtags, but also tag your own tweets so that others can find your tweets when they search by hashtags. Third, hashtags are great for chatting. Educators can use the same hashtag to chat and plan to meet online at a scheduled time. Here is a list of educationally focused chats that are recommended by Edutopia (Ray, 2012).

Chat for educators teaching fourth grade #4thchat

Mondays, 8 p.m. ET/5 p.m. PT

Chat for educators teaching social studies #sschat

Mondays, 7 p.m. ET/4 p.m. PT

Chat for music educators #musedchat

Mondays, 8 p.m. ET/5 p.m. PT

Chat for educators of English language learners #ellchat

Mondays, 9 p.m. ET/6 p.m. PT

Kindergarten chat #kinderchat

Mondays, 9 p.m. ET/6 p.m. PT

General education chat #edchat

Tuesdays, 12 noon ET/9 a.m. PT; 7 p.m. ET/4 p.m. PT

Chat for science educators #scichat

Tuesdays, 9 p.m. ET/6 p.m. PT

Chat for new and preservice teachers #ntchat

Wednesdays, 8 p.m. ET/5 p.m. PT

Chat for parents and teachers #ptchat

Wednesdays, 9 p.m. ET/6 p.m. PT

Chat for arts educators #artsed

Thursdays, 7 p.m. ET/4 p.m. PT

Chat for educators teaching world languages #langchat

Thursdays, 8 p.m. ET/5 p.m. PT

Chat for educators teaching at the elementary level #elemchat

Saturdays, 5 p.m. ET (U.S.)/7 a.m. Sunday (Sydney, Australia)

Pinterest

Pinterest is another great PLN tool. It is a tool for collecting and organizing things that you love, as described on its homepage. Users create and share collections (called "boards") of visual bookmarks (called "pins"). The themes of the boards vary from birthday party plans to recipes. Examples of topics of educational boards are educational technology, project-based learning, flipped classroom, children's literature, and so on. When you pin a resource, you will get alerts about who else has marked that resource, which makes it much easier to find who may share your interests. When you like the pins on a board, you can follow the board. By following, new pins on the board will be fed to you. You may also be followed by people who find your pins interesting and helpful. You are developing your own PLN by following other boards and getting your own followers. When you view others' pins, you can repost ("repin") the pin, leave a comment on the board, or click to like the pin. Under each pin, you will see statistics—number of reposts, number of likes it has collected, and number of comments it has received. You can also share your board and invite others to create the board with you.

Collaboration

Technology can also bring collaboration to a totally new level. Collaboration is no longer limited between you and someone you already know. You could reach a much wider public audience if you want. All the above PLN examples illustrate how you could collaborate with people who share your professional interests but probably have not met you before. For example, if you are interested in Web 2.0, social media, and technologies in the classroom, you could become a member of Classroom 2.0 (www.classroom20.com). As a member of this social media platform for teachers, you can share your insights in a forum where other teacher members can see your posts and give you feedback. When you have questions and want to get help from other teachers, post your questions in the forum and your questions may be answered. Another great example is PenPal Projects, in which students communicate with students in another country and share their ideas and thoughts. Students could use emails, blogs, wikis, and social media tools such as Edmodo to reach their counterparts in their PenPal projects.

Collaboration with people you already know also looks a whole lot different now. For example, class communication is no longer just conversations in the classroom during class time. Students can write collaboratively in a Google Doc, with different students writing different sections of the paper at the same time, viewing all the changes that others have made in the same document, and making further revisions as needed. Students can also collaborate with each other via online video conferencing tools such as Skype or Google Hangout. Asynchronous tools (e.g., online threaded discussion) provide an additional channel for peer communication.

Collaborative tools such as Google Docs, Google Hangout, and Skype work well not only for students, but also for teachers and educators. Teachers and educators can easily share their lesson plans, rubrics, assessments, and other instruction materials via Google Docs. When they share, they need to enter their colleagues' email addresses and can choose if they want to invite their colleges to just view the document or to edit it as well. Google Hangout, Skype, and Voxer are free tools that can be used for small-group communication. Google Hangout and Skype support small-group chatting and videoconferencing. Voxer is, simply put, a walkie-talkie application. Different from traditional walkie-talkie radios that you probably have seen in schools buildings, Voxer allows educators to chat with educators all over the world. Users can send text messages, pictures, and instant voice messages to individuals and groups. School administrators can use this app to supplement their use of traditional walkie-talkie radios with staff and teachers. Some school districts use Voxer to help teachers stay connected with other teachers in the district. On a broader level, Voxer enables a teacher to connect to other teachers in the world and send/receive text messages, voice messages, and pictures.

iLearn

The most profound change that technology brings to learning is probably the possibility of developing a new learning model, the iLearn model, which encompasses two key features: personalized instruction (the "i" part) and an active role played by learners (the "Learn" part).

While accommodating learners' individual needs has been around for a while, it is not often what is really going on in the classroom. The truth is, it is a daunting task to find out and then accommodate the individual needs of a group of 20 or more students. Students' individual needs include, but are not limited to,

- different instruction levels
- different first languages spoken at home
- different learning styles

The list can go on. But it already seems overwhelming. While it is still not an easy task to accommodate all of those needs, technology can be a great help.

Different Instruction Levels

Technology can be helpful in identifying different instruction levels for students and then providing differentiated instruction based on a learner's instruction level. Accommodating different instruction levels requires identifying each student's instruction level. Technology-based assessment such as Google Forms makes it easier to distribute assessment, auto-grade assessment, and analyze results. Teachers can then design learning activities for learners according to the results of the assessment. Technology can also help teachers provide appropriate learning materials and activities for students at different levels. Pearl Diver, a free math application developed by a university to teach the number line, is a good example. The app is geared for students in Grades 3–8. Learners dive for hidden pearls within the number line. What makes the app adaptive to learners' levels is that the difficulty level increases after every successful dive. Such a feature is now embedded in many applications and educational games. Teachers can also manually adjust the difficulty level.

Different First Languages Spoken at Home

When teachers have English language learners in their class, communicating with these students and their parents becomes a challenge. It would be a lot easier if the teacher happens to speak a family's language or the school has access to parent volunteers who speak that language. However, chances are the teacher probably doesn't speak the language, nor could he or she find help from parent volunteers all the time. Translator technology such as Google Translate, iSpeak Spanish, or iTranslate can be useful. For instance, iTranslate translates words and whole words in sentences in 52 languages and uses text to speech with 43 voices in 16 languages. With Google Translate, teachers can even speak phrases and hear the corresponding translations.

Different Learning Styles

Learners may prefer different learning styles, which is another layer of personalized instruction. There are seven learning styles—visual, auditory-musical, linguistic, kinesthetic, mathematical, interpersonal, and intrapersonal. Technology provides more opportunities to meet these learning styles. With a variety of Web 2.0 tools that are easy to use and share, learners can be presented with many opportunities to choose their preferred format of work (e.g., audio recording, essay, visual presentations) that may better meet their learning styles. Teachers can also select various ways to present instruction materials. For example, podcasts can be provided for auditory-musical learners, e-books can be used for linguistic learners, and visual presentations (such as infographics) may greatly help visual learners.

One feature of the iLearn model is that learners take an active role in their learning. The affordances of technology provide more and richer opportunities than ever before for learners to be active. With enormous numbers of free resources (e.g., books, videos, simulations, tutorials) available online, learners can assume many more responsibilities in their learning. Learners can search for additional learning materials and tutorials, create digital flashcards to help them remember key concepts, view simulations to gain contextualized knowledge, and play interactive games to test their knowledge. Learners could even take free massive open online courses (MOOCs). In addition, learners can create and maintain their own learning networks. By publishing and sharing their work online, learners can seek feedback and suggestions from people outside their immediate network, which was not possible in the past.

Dr. Sugata Mitra's "A Hole in the Wall" is a perfect example of the active role learners can play when learning with technology (Hole-in-the-Wall Education, 2013). Dr. Sugata Mitra, an educational researcher from India, demonstrated the value of educational technology to the world in a distinctive way. In his well-known "A Hole in the Wall" experiment, he and his colleagues dug a hole in a wall in an urban slum in New Delhi, installed an Internet-connected computer, and left it there (with a hidden camera filming the area and showing his research team what the children were doing with the computer). His research team was amazed at what they saw. Kids from the slum were playing with the computer, they were learning how to use it and how to go online, and they taught each other. The video feed showed that children were recording music and playing it back for each other within only 4 hours of seeing the computer for the first time. Dr. Mitra repeated the experiment in other parts in India and discovered that children learn what they want to do and computers play a big role in facilitating students' individual needs in learning.

Digital textbooks, personal learning networks, better collaboration, personalized learning experience, and more power for learners are just a few examples of how technology can facilitate learning. In their book *Using Technology With Classroom Instruction That Works,* Pitler, Hubbell, and Kuhn (2012) systematically reviewed technology tools that go well with Marzano's nine essential instructional strategies (Marzano, Pickering, & Pollock, 2001):

1. Setting objectives and providing feedback

2. Reinforcing effort and providing recognition

3. Cooperative learning

4. Cues, questions, and advance organizers

5. Nonlinguistic representations

6. Summarizing and note taking

7. Assigning homework and providing practice

8. Identifying similarities and differences

9. Generating and testing hypotheses

As suggested by these examples, computers can play a great role in teaching and learning, but only if we really unleash its potential and do not limit its role in improving test scores. As George Siemens (2011, pp. 8–9) puts it:

If it changes how information is created

If it changes how information is shared

If it changes how information is evaluated . . .

If it changes how people connect

If it changes how people communicate

If it changes what people can do for themselves . . .

Then it will change education, teaching and learning.

And that should be the charge of technology in learning.

REFERENCES

Berler, R. (2013). *Raising the curve: A year inside one of America's 45,000 failing public schools.* New York, NY: Penguin.

Cattell, R. B. (1971). *Abilities: Their structure, growth, and action.* Boston, MA: Houghton Mifflin.

Entwisle, D. R., Alexander, K. L., & Olson, L. S. (2005). Urban teenagers: Work and dropout. *Youth and Society, 37*(1), 3–32.

Fitzgerald, J. (2013, December 22). NY school all-in on trend of all-digital textbooks. *Huffington Post.* Retrieved from http://www.huffingtonpost .com

Heckman, J. J., Stixrud, J., & Urzua, S. (2006). The effects of cognitive and noncognitive abilities on labor market outcomes and social behavior. *Journal of Labor Economics, 24,* 411–482.

Hole-in-the-Wall Education. (2013). *Hole-in-the-wall: Lighting the spark of learning.* Retrieved from http://www.hole-in-the-wall.com

Hu, W. (2007, May 4). Seeing no progress, some schools drop laptop. *New York Times.* Retrieved from http://www.nytimes.com

Louie, K. (2013, October 15). Interactive textbooks revolutionizing the classroom text. *EmergingTech.* Retrieved from http://www.emerging edtech.com

Marzano, R. J., Pickering, D. J., & Pollock, J. E. (2001). *Classroom instruction that works: Research-based strategies for increasing student achievement.* Alexandria, VA: Association for Supervision and Curriculum Development.

Maslow, A. H. (1966). *The psychology of science: A reconnaissance.* New York, NY: Harper & Row.

Massachusetts Institute of Technology. (2013, December 11). Even when test scores go up, some cognitive abilities don't. *ScienceDaily.* Retrieved from http://www.sciencedaily.com

National Center for Education Statistics. (2011). *TIMSS 2011 results.* Retrieved from http://nces.ed.gov/timss/results11.asp

Nelson, H. (2013). *Testing more, teaching less: What America's obsession with student testing costs in money and lost instructional time.* Washington, DC: American Federation of Teachers. Retrieved from http://www.aft.org/pdfs/teachers/testingmore2013.pdf

Norris, C., & Soloway, E. (2012, July/August). Want increased student achievement using iPads? *District Administration.* Retrieved from http://www.districtadministration.com

Pitler, H., Hubbell, E. R., & Kuhn, M. (2012). *Using technology with classroom instruction that works.* Alexandria, VA: Association for Supervision and Curriculum Development.

Ray, B. (2012, December 7). How to use Twitter to grow your PLN. *Edutopia.* Retrieved from http://www.edutopia.org

Richtel, M. (2011, September 3). In classroom of future, stagnant scores. *New York Times.* Retrieved from http://www.nytimes.com

Rosen, J. A., Glennie, E. J., Dalton, B. W., Lennon, J. M., & Bozick, R. N. (2010). *Noncognitive skills in the classroom: New perspective on educational research.* Triangle Park, NC: RTI Press.

Segal, C. (2008). Classroom behavior. *Journal of Human Resources, 43,* 783–814.

Siemens, G. (2011). *At the threshold: Higher education, complexity, and change.* Retrieved from http://www.slideshare.net/gsiemens/unisa-south-africa

Soloway, E., & Norris, C. (2013, January 9). Realizing increased student achievement with mobile technologies: Here's the plan. *THE Journal.* Retrieved from http://thejournal.com

Tomaszewski, J. (2012). Mobile apps and devices increase student achievement. *EducationWorld.* Retrieved from http://www.education world.com

CHAPTER FOUR

The Wrong Assumptions

Technology as Curriculum Versus Digital Competence

As an enterprise that prepares a competent workforce for tomorrow's job market, the education system worldwide is now facing an unprecedented challenge: Tomorrow is very difficult, if not impossible, to predict. Nobody knows for sure what tomorrow's job market will be like and thus what kind of workforce will be needed and most valued. For hundreds of years, schools have been adequately successful in preparing whatever talents their society needed, largely because human society had been progressing very slowly and in almost invisible ways, and dramatic changes were rare within a few generations. For nearly the entire human history, the future was not much different from the present. However, in the last few decades, the rapid advancement and exponential growth of information and communication technology (ICT) has been dramatically changing society, so dramatically and rapidly that some scholars claim that the world is flat (Friedman, 2005), distance is dead (Cairncross & Cairncross, 2001), and we are now entering the future that, as Alvin Toffler (1984) predicted more than 30 years ago, is characterized by "too much change in too short a period of time" (p. 2).

Compared with the amount of change, the nature of the change brought about by technology is having even more significant impacts on society and on the ways we live and work. Technology is quickly surpassing human beings in terms of efficiency, effectiveness, and cost-saving in more and more areas. Today's technology not only can beat chess grandmasters and win *Jeopardy* games, but also can drive cars, talk to people, and write a scientific conference paper (Brynjolfsson & McAfee, n.d.). Technology is devaluing many skills deemed necessary or indispensable in previous generations, making it inevitable that some people will lose their jobs to new technology. In fact, many people have already lost their jobs due to automation or outsourcing (Pink, 2005). The scope of the changes is not limited to jobs considered easy to replace, such as those in manufacturing, but extends to more and more areas. According to a recent McKinsey Global Institute report, disruptive technologies are transforming life, business, and the global economy, challenging professionals even with highly educated skills (Manyika et al., 2013). This trend is going to continue and even accelerate, making it necessary for people to change careers during their lifetime.

Then how can schools sufficiently prepare competent workers for occupations that don't yet exist or that are going to change? What are the essential skills, knowledge, and abilities that students must acquire to successfully live and work in an ever-changing world? What talents will be most useful and valued?

As Brynjolfsson and McAfee (n.d.) point out, "there's never been a worse time to be a worker with only 'ordinary' skills and abilities to offer, because computers, robots, and other digital technologies are acquiring these skills and abilities at an extraordinary rate" (p. 9). Yet schools are still working hard to focus on mostly the traditional "ordinary" skills to produce standardized laborers. In doing so, the more effective our education system is, the less competent and competitive our next generation of workforce becomes, as we are setting students up for a "race against the machine" (Brynjolfsson & McAfee, n.d.). When people compete against the machines, based on what we learned from the Industrial Revolution, the results might not be positive for the individual workers.

THE WRONG ASSUMPTIONS: TECHNOLOGY AS CURRICULUM/INSTRUCTION

It is well acknowledged that since ICT has been the driving force behind these dramatic, rapid, and revolutionary changes, it is reasonable to suggest that the abilities to understand and use technology, to successfully live and work in an ever-changing technological society, are what constitute the most fundamental competence that tomorrow's workers need.

What that competence entails and how to prepare students with such competence has been a central topic in education discourse and reform efforts in the last two decades. Depending on assumptions about the role of technology, there are different approaches to how to prepare children to be fully technology competent. The traditional approach that the school system has been taking is the one that views technology mostly as a tool, and thus teaching technology as a subject through instruction.

Schools have been teaching technology as curriculum since the very early days when technology was first introduced into schools. Although computers entered schools as early as the 1960s, they were mostly used for research purposes or for administration tasks. In the 1970s and early 1980s, technology in schools was viewed as a subject; students were expected to study the machine and learn specific skills to make the technology work. The title of Robert Taylor's (1980) book *The Computer in the School: Tutor, Tool, Tutee* depicts the three types of uses of computers. In a review of how computers have been used in schools in the last 30 years, Luehrmann (2002) summarizes computer use according to Taylor's trichotomy and concludes that the only impact that computers had on schools was as a teaching tool, while they were used very limitedly as tutee and as tutor. In the late 1980s and early 1990s, with the outbreak of personal computers and user-friendly graphical user interface, computer education experienced a dramatic growth. Computers were viewed as a supplement to teaching and learning, and curriculum-based software was developed and introduced into schools. Computer courses mainly focused on specific skills such as keyboarding and word processing. In the late 1990s, the rapid development of the Internet stimulated another dramatic growth of interest and a tremendous shift of content in computer education. Schools began to teach networking, Web surfing, webpage development, email, in addition to multimedia tools. Conlon (2000) points out that the discourse of technology in education is mostly at the technical and craft levels.

Entering the 21st century, with the increasingly ubiquitous access to technology and popular use of technology among young students, technology education in schools has been in a somewhat awkward situation. While technology literacy is well recognized by educators as an important area, often technology classes in schools still focus mainly on the teaching and learning of handcraft skills (de Vries, 2011, p. 1). Although some specific ICT content has been added to technology classes, overall there is a lack of technology education focused on deep understanding of the science of technology (George, 2014).

Viewing technology mostly as a tool and teaching technology as a curriculum, the resulting practices of educational technologies are defective, and very likely detrimental, for preparing children for the future. First, new educational technologies are emerging every day, and it has become impossible to keep up with new technologies, let alone to provide professional development for teachers to learn these technologies and then transfer their knowledge to students. A 2009 Cisco research synthesis points out that one of the five major miscalculations of educators in terms of technology is "in underestimating the rate of change in technology, and the impact of such rapid, continuous change on staff time, budgeting, professional development, software upgrades, and curricular and lesson redesign" (Lemke, Coughlin, & Reifsneider, 2009, p. 5). As a result, "schools are forever playing technological catch up as digital innovations emerge" (Editorial Projects in Education Research Center, 2011). Also, because technologies are changing extremely quickly, many will become obsolete soon after students learn them.

Second, viewing technology only as a tool omits the value that technology offers when it is used in different contexts and for different purposes, and thus the social, cultural, and legal implications that may arise in such usage. Technology is not culturally neutral. Cultures vary in their receptivity to technology, and technology carries different connotations in different cultures. The same technology may be perceived to carry different social connotations to people in different cultures and thus is responded to differently.

Third, there is less demand among young students to learn technology as mostly a tool, because today's students are much more technology-savvy than previous generations. In fact, the reality is that students often know much more about technology than their teachers do. One-third of the teachers who participated in a 2013 survey agreed that "I like the idea of using new technology, but often the kids know more than I do" (VeraQuest, 2013, p. 15). In some schools, technology-savvy students even provide technology support to their teachers. What is needed is to help the digital natives develop a deep understanding of the nature of technology and the social, cultural, and legal impact of technology.

Furthermore, as mentioned at the beginning of the chapter, focusing on technology as a tool and teaching technology as a curriculum only prepares workers with "ordinary" skills—skills that technology can easily learn and be better at, and thus put the workers with such skills out of work. At a time when technology use involves less and less technical skill and programing knowledge, technology education still centers on introduction to various technology tools and software. Digital competence, a set of new knowledge and skills required to thrive in this global and technological world, is unfortunately ignored and under-taught.

WHAT IS DIGITAL CITIZENSHIP?

Instead of teaching one technology tool after another, technology education should focus on preparing competent digital citizens. Today's young people must take the role of contributing members and creative leaders in the virtual world, and education needs to provide a world-class capable workforce that is digital literate, independent, and creative. Most important, learning to live in a world of technology and constant change is itself a valuable goal of using technology in schools.

Digital citizenship is the ability to live in the digital world productively and be a contributing member to society. It includes the following fundamental elements: (a) knowledge of the nature of the digital world, (b) positive attitude toward the digital world, (c) ability to use different tools to participate in the digital world, and (d) ability to use different tools to create digital products and to lead in the digital world.

Knowledge of the Nature of the Digital World

A digital citizen is an intelligent digital consumer who understands the nature of the digital world, including the differences and connections between the physical and virtual worlds, the nature of technology and how different media work together, the nature of online/virtual activities, the nature of the digital world as a constantly expanding and evolving global network of individual and collective participants, and the ability to tell fantasy from reality.

Understand That the Digital World Is Ever Growing and Expanding

Technology is changing society in two ways. First, our traditional physical world is being increasingly digitized. The economy worldwide is increasingly driven by technology. An analysis based on 2010 data from the Bureau of Labor Statistics reveals that ICT directly supported nearly 11 million high-paying jobs in the United States, and this number will grow by 1.3 to 1.5 million more jobs in 10 years (Brogan, 2012). The use of mobile devices has also increasingly digitized our physical world. ComScore (2014) reports that the number of smartphone users grew 24% in 2013 to 156 million owners in December 2013, reaching 65% mobile market penetration, and tablet adoption grew 57% to 82 million owners, which means that one out of every three mobile users has a tablet. This report further points out that the amount of time Americans spent on the Internet doubled in the last 3 years.

Second, the growth of the online world has been dramatic in terms of both the content and structure of the online world and our engagement in it. In June 2014, Cisco Visual Networking Index (VNI), an ongoing initiative to track and forecast the impact of visual networking applications, reported that global internet protocol (IP) traffic grew more than five times in the previous 5 years and predicted that it will increase threefold in the next 5 years, and by 2018, global IP traffic will reach1.6 zettabytes per year, or 131.6 exabytes per month (one exabyte is 1,000 million gigabytes, and five exabytes would equal a text transcript of all words ever spoken in the world; Cisco, 2014a). The online population also has grown rapidly, from about 361 million Internet users worldwide in 2000 to more than 2.8 billion in 2013, a 676.3% growth rate, and Internet penetration rate has reached 85% in North America (Internet World Stats, 2014). The number of Internet users is predicted to reach 3.6 billion by 2017 (Cisco, 2014b).

Understand the Blurring Boundaries Between Real and Virtual

The boundaries between the real and the virtual are blurring. The real is a part of virtual, and virtual is real. First, there is less and less distinction between our identities in the virtual world and in the physical world. With the increasingly popular usage of Web 2.0 technology, and particularly the ubiquitous use of social networking media, people are combining their online persona with their real-life true identity. What we present online is part of what we are in real life. People's online friends are often their real-life buddies. This is particularly so for the younger generation. Called the "App Generation" by Howard Gardner and Katie Davis (2013), they feel very differently from previous generations about issues such as privacy and identity, and are often very generous with sharing whatever they want to share.

Second, researchers have found that social norms that work in real life are also being applied in the virtual world. For example, in an observational study of Second Life, a group of researchers collected data on how avatars interact with each other in terms of three social norms in real life: gender, interpersonal distance, and eye gaze. By observing the verbal and nonverbal behaviors of avatars, they found that even though the movement modality is totally different, these social norms exist in Second Life and are followed by its residents, and the "congruency of social norms in Second Life and the real world are quite striking" (Yee, Bailenson, Urbanek, Chang, & Merget, 2007, p. 119).

Third, virtual actions have real consequences, including both good consequences such as YouTube businesses and bad consequences such as online victimization. Virtual earnings in cyberspace can lead to real economic gains and thus, in some situations, real taxes. Apart from e-commerce, many people have made profits or even made a living from their activities in virtual worlds. One can make money in the digital world, and one can also lose money. For example, in 2008, financial missteps in one of Second Life's virtual banks caused an estimated loss of $750,000 in real money of its users (Sidel, 2008).

Understand the Opportunities and Potential Risks

The digital world is full of new opportunities as well as potential risks. On the one hand, the Internet presents new opportunities for business and new ways to work and entertain. In 2013, Americans spent approximately $263 billion online, a 16.9% of growth from the previous year, much higher than the average growth rate of overall retail sales, and this amount is projected to reach more than $491.5 billion by 2018 ("Total US Retail Sales," 2014). This is a global trend. In China, 20% of cosmetics sales took place online, compared to 5% in the United States, and in Nigeria, the "e-commerce market has grown 25% annually pretty consistently, and is beginning to have a significant impact on the country's GDP" (Smith, 2014, para. 7).

On the other hand, there are new challenges and potential dangers such as privacy concerns, online victimization, and cybercrime. A 2012 survey found that nearly one in five Americans reported being victimized online; the biggest concerns related to children were adult sexual content (39%), making contact with strangers (27%), bullying or harassment from peers (10%), and identify theft (9%; National Cyber Security Alliance, 2013). There have been several high-profile lawsuits against online bullies whose victimizing behavior cause great damage, sometimes even death, in their victims (e.g., "Missouri Woman Indicted," 2008). The recent Snapchat photo leak incident demonstrated how vulnerable technology users can be even with the supposedly most private chat program. Snapchat, an instant photo-sharing chat app, gained immense popularity in the last few years due to the ephemeral nature of its photo messaging content, as photos shared via the app are not stored. This nature has great appeal among mostly teenage users, knowing that whatever they send over this app will disappear. However, in October 2014, news broke that hackers had access to at least 100,000 Snapchat photos. A third-party app had been collecting every single Snapchat photo and video that users thought had been deleted (Cook, 2014). Cybercrime is also becoming an increasingly serious threat online. According to a recent McAfee report, in 2013, online hackers stole personal information from an estimated total of more than 800 million people around the world. It was guessed that the likely annual cost to the global economy from cybercrime is more than $400 billion (McAfee, 2014). Young people are also at risk of getting involved in committing cybercrimes without an understanding of the consequences. Many recent news stories have reported that teen technology geniuses hacked into government or other institutions' websites or databases, often resulting in being charged and potentially facing jail time ("Teen Hackers," 2012).

For young people to responsibly participate in the online world, they need to understand the ever-changing nature of the digital world as well as both the opportunities and the potential risks of online participation. Meanwhile, they also need to participate responsibly and not contribute to online risks.

As technology continues to advance rapidly, one can only expect that technology is going to further digitize our world and interact with every aspect of our work and life. With this understanding, a digital citizen is able to face the uncertainty and expect changes that technology brings, prepare to adapt to the changes, and, more important, become part of the change.

Positive Attitude Toward the Digital World

The ever-expanding and ever-changing nature of the digital world is exciting as well as confusing and frustrating at times. Competent digital citizens must be able to understand the complexity of the digital world, develop an appreciation of the complexity and uncertainty of the digital world, and prepare effective strategies to approach technical problems and to learn new ways of communicating and sharing information.

Attitudes play an important role in determining whether people's reactions to certain situations are favorable or unfavorable. Research has identified attitudes as a critical factor in teachers' technology decision-making process (i.e., Al-Zaidiyeen, Mei, & Fook, 2010; Sabizan & Gilakjani, 2013). Since attitude is "a learned predisposition" (Fishbein & Ajzen, 1975, p. 6), it can be changed, unlearned, and relearned.

Our attitudes toward change may not be positive and can even be negative at times. During the Industrial Revolution, the invention of the steam engine and the use of machines brought unprecedented production power, but this was viewed by the workers as a great threat to their survival. In fear of their jobs being replaced by the machines, some workers even destroyed the machines. What happened later proved that their fear was not unfounded: The machines indeed replaced workers on many jobs. The Industrial Revolution led to significant improvement in living standards, but many workers within the first few generations were clearly hurt as they were thrown out of work by their much more powerful competitor, the machines, and the workers hurt the most were those whose acquired skills were suddenly devalued by the machines (Krugman, 2013).

More than 200 years later, we are facing a similar situation, only the transformative power of ICT is even greater than that of the steam engine. Modern ICT not only brings constant changes, but also is quickly surpassing human beings in more and more areas, making it inevitable that many people will lose their jobs to new technology. It is likely that people will have one career after another, and hence the need to continue to learn.

So how do we stay positive when facing such challenges? The first key to this question is understanding: understanding the nature of technology, understanding both the opportunities and challenges that technology presents, and understanding what technology can do best and what human beings can do better. Fear comes from the unknown. Through understanding the nature of technology, digital citizens can develop an appreciation of the complexity and uncertainty of the digital world. When users understand the diverse nature of the vast digital universe, they can also develop an appreciation of this diversity and work well with others online or offline.

The second key is practicing: learning and doing with technology. Through working with technology, we test our comfort zone and explore new territories, gaining new experiences, confidence, and more understanding with technology. As Charles F. Glassman points out, "Fear and anxiety many times indicates that we are moving in a positive direction, out of the safe confines of our comfort zone, and in the direction of our true purpose" (cited by Loyland, 2014, "Closing Thoughts," para. 2). Research has found that positive attitudes and technology use support each other: Teachers and students with positive attitudes toward technology have a higher level of ICT usage, and those who use technology more often show positive attitude toward technology (Al-Zaidiyeen et al., 2010; Tubaishat, 2014).

With practice, people can also develop effective strategies to work with technology and to creatively solve technical problems. For example, technology often breaks, and when this happens, it is important to know where and how to obtain resources and assistance. Technology itself provides such a platform for people to seek help. Nowadays we rely on technology to help us make the most of our decisions, from which house to buy and where to take a vacation to what movie to watch on a Friday night. The more we work with technology, the more likely we are to develop effective strategies to approach technical problems and to learn new ways of communicating and sharing information.

Ability to Use Different Tools to Participate in the Digital World

Competent digital citizens must have the abilities to use various technology tools to fully participate in the digital world, including finding and sharing information; entertaining, learning, working; and obtaining and sharing information; and collaborating with others.

First, regarding the abilities to find reliable sources of information, the reality is that in the zettabyte era (Cisco, 2014a), there is an overload of information. A search of any term could bring up millions of entries. Without the necessary skills for proper Internet searching, it is very easy to get lost in this vast universe. Another challenge is finding reliable information. The tricky side of online resources is that anyone with Internet access and the necessary computer skills can offer information online, and anything can be published online regardless of its quality and credibility. In a Pew Research Center project, high school teachers reported that the Internet and digital technologies had multifaceted and complex impacts on student learning, as the Internet opens up vast resources for students, yet also requires students to dig through the immensity to find credible and reliable information (Purcell et al., 2012). Therefore, it is crucial to be able to not only locate resources online but, more important, discern the quality and credibility of online resources.

Second, regarding the abilities to entertain, learn, work, and obtain and share information in the digital world, digital citizens are not just the "users" of the Internet; instead, we must actively participate in creating, making, and remaking the digital world. Various websites, software, and apps make it possible for users to obtain and share information through a variety of media: searchable databases, digital storytelling, blogging, podcasting, discussion forums, social networking, social media, mobile phone, and wikis. We have been witnessing the growing trend of digital natives actively contributing digital content. For example, the use of apps is very common among teenagers. The 2013 Speak Up project reported that 44% of students in Grades 6–12 use social media apps such as Instagram, Snapchat, and Vine, and nearly one-third of high school students reported using Twitter (Project Tomorrow, 2014). YouTube has become a major media source for information and entertainment, reaching more U.S. adults ages 18–34 than any cable network. At the same time, users are also creators of YouTube content, with most of the videos uploaded by individual users.

Third, we have the ability to competently collaborate with others. Being able to collaboratively work with others has become an increasingly important ability for anyone working and living in the digital world, as modern ICT has shrunk the world into a global village in which we are interconnected and interdependent with each other. Most of today's issues or projects require collaborative efforts. For example, at the national level, governments around the world must work together to face some of the most urgent threats such as terrorism, climate change, famine, and pandemics. The current outbreak of Ebola is one such example that requires collaboration among nations, organizations, and institutions. Today's students, growing up with technology and immersed in social networking interactions, are naturally enthusiastic about using collaborative technologies to participate in the digital world. They participate as creators rather than consumers, and they "gravitate toward group activity, seeking interaction within thriving online communities of generative individuals" (Rosen & Nelson, 2008, p. 220).

Ability to Use Different Tools to Create Digital Products and to Lead in the Digital World

Invention and Innovation: Creatively Contribute to the Digital World

Creativity has been the driving force behind every social and technological progress, including the rapid advancement of ICT. Innovation has been critical to economic growth. In the digital world, creative thinking and creative problem solving are not only key to success, but also crucial to the survival of most people as we are presented with new opportunities and face the new challenges technology brings about. Citizens must also be able to contribute to the digital world by innovatively creating digital products and services and creating, managing, and leading online communities. Modern ICT provides the necessary tools and platforms for young people to create and share their digital products online. Apps such as Instagram, Snapchat, and Vine, with their highly visual and easily digestible content, are very appealing to young people and make content creation especially convenient and compelling, providing the fuel that has led to high-intensity interaction and the rapid growth of these platforms (ComScore, 2014).

The abilities to create digital products and services and share or sell their products are essential to entrepreneurs in the digital world. The Internet provides the platform for any content creator to easily reach millions of people at once or to reach targeted groups of people even if they are dispersed around the world. In addition, the Internet and the growing resources it offers provide unlimited opportunities for creation and invention. For example, the Internet and free and open source software have made it possible not only for more user-driven innovation to happen, but also for these individual creations to diffuse through networks of like-minded individuals (Benkler, 2006).

Creativity is the most sought-after quality in students around the world, yet the irony is that schools don't teach creativity; instead, they kill it (Zhao, 2006). To improve the situation and to ensure that schools at least preserve creativity, educators must be given the autonomy to innovate with an entrepreneurial spirit. There are many entrepreneurship courses and programs being offered in colleges and universities to help students gain creative invention experiences. However, current entrepreneurship education often defines entrepreneurship too narrowly, focusing on the short-term economic return and leaving out alternative ways of innovation (Clark, 2013). To nurture creativity and invention, children need to be exposed to entrepreneurship education from very early on, and to different styles of creativity, so that they can explore their own potential and interests as designers, creators, and entrepreneurs.

Effectively Lead in the Digital World

Digital leadership is needed when we try to regulate cyberspace and form functional online communities. The online world has been growing exponentially, yet regulation of online activities has been struggling to keep up. The virtual world has become the "Digital Wild West" (Schneiderman, 2014). However, as online activities continue to play an increasingly important role, regulating the virtual world is in urgent need. Whether social norms in real life apply in the virtual world has been debated, and the different viewpoints can be roughly grouped into three categories: the *exceptionalists* who believe that the virtual world is fundamentally different from the real world and thus should be governed by its own rules and regulations, the *unexceptionalists* who believe that the virtual world is no different from the real world and thus should be governed by the same rules and regulations that apply to the real world, and the *middle ground* that recognizes the virtual world as a distinct world based on the theory of "code is law" and at the same time recognizes the need for real-world intervention when the code fails to protect the virtual world (Stoup, 2008).

These different viewpoints have been tested by researchers. Stoup (2008) says that although some evidence suggests that social norms in real life are present in virtual worlds, there are technical and practical barriers that make it difficult to maximize the welfare of the residents; therefore, it is necessary for members of the online community to work together to figure out how to break the barriers and best regulate online activities. Lessig (2000, 2006) argues not only that cyberspace is regulable and needs regulation, but more important, the citizens of cyberspace must take steps to get involved in the process of forming regulations, shaping what kind of regulations we need and want for cyberspace and, hence, what kind of cyberspace we will have.

DEVELOPING DIGITAL CITIZENSHIP THROUGH THE USE OF DIGITAL TECHNOLOGY

Digital citizenship is a multifaceted set of knowledge, attitudes, skills, and abilities that can only be developed by actually working with digital technology. Around the world young people are using various digital technology, exploring the vast possibilities, and gaining experiences and maturity in the digital world.

For example, immensely popular among young people, social networking media provides a platform for students to engage in various digital activities and has shown great potential to prepare students for digital citizenship. Using a variety of applications, particularly those highly visual apps on their mobile devices that enable instant sharing and instant participation, young people lead in the use of almost every social media, including Instagram, Vine, Snapchat, and Pinterest. For example, according to reports from the Pew Internet Research Project, only 19% of adult Internet users use Twitter, while 24% of teenagers do. Teenagers also lead the use of Snapchat. As of May 2014, Snapchat users were sending 700 million photos and videos per day, up from 60 million per day in February 2013 (Shontell, 2014).

Social media has become the most important venue for young people to express themselves, share information, and communicate with peers. A 2013 Pew Internet survey reported that teens are sharing much more information about themselves on social media than they ever did before. A typical teen Facebook user has 300 friends, and a typical teen Twitter user has 79 followers; and they often have positive attitudes and experiences with their online activities (Madden et al., 2013).

Using social media requires multiple forms of creation. For example, using Twitter involves the composition of one's thoughts and ideas in a very concise way, and the use of Vine requires taking a short video and sharing it with others. On Pinterest, users can create digital bulletin boards related to particular themes, and they can use the boards to work on projects, organize events, and discover, collect, and save resources.

Social media can also serve as a constructive learning context where students work collaboratively on projects, interact with their teacher and peers, and build a collegial culture for learning and social interactions. For example, in one study, low-income high school students used social networking sites for self-discovery, self-presentation, identity exploration, and specifically for learning 21st-century skills. By using different technology features such as photo sharing, graphic design, and multiple communication channels, students indicated that they gained technical skills and began to consider their role as responsible citizens in the digital world (Greenhow & Robelia, 2009).

Using social media, young people also engage in democratic discourses and citizenship participation online. Nearly two-thirds of students report using social networking to discuss topics such as politics, religion, and morals (National School Boards Association, 2007). Their online civic engagement can have real effects. Wylie and Marri (2010) documented such a case in Kenny High School, in Florida. Upon witnessing an injustice committed by the school's administration against one of their fellow classmates, students actively engaged in heated discussions on Facebook, using the tools of democracy to voice their displeasure and suggesting how to act to resolve this particular issue and to fix the system. Their online campaign was effective enough to make school administrators give the particular student a second chance. Through this process, students demonstrated their enthusiasm about democratic participation and the initiative to lead in social and political affairs.

New technology innovations are being developed every day, and students are leading the way in adopting the new technology and using it in ways they see fit. The best that schools and adults can do to help in this process is to understand and encourage participation, inspire curiosity and interest, and provide support and guidance when needed. The National School Boards Association (2011) advocates that, despite safety concerns, schools should consider the advantages of social media for learning. Instead of limiting the use of social media and mobile devices, schools need to provide the opportunity for students to explore in a safe environment with adult supervision and gain the abilities to eventually act competently and responsibly on their own.

As digital technologies continue to accelerate, the only thing we can be certain about in terms of tomorrow's society and job market is their uncertainty. How to prepare the next generation of citizens to be able to deal with the uncertainty, adapt to constant changes, and live a happy and fulfilling life is today's grand challenge. Schools are at the forefront facing this challenge, because what kind of education students receive today will, to a great degree, determine their life and career in tomorrow's society.

The title of this book suggests that we should never send a human to do a machine's job. Similarly, schools should never prepare citizens to compete against technology. Instead, we need to think differently about our relationship with technology, encourage positive attitudes toward change, nurture creativity and an entrepreneurial spirit, develop the abilities to face the unknown, and prepare lifelong learners who can adapt to the ever-evolving digital world.

REFERENCES

Al-Zaidiyeen, N. J., Mei, L. L., & Fook, F. S. (2010). Teachers' attitudes and levels of technology use in classrooms: The case of Jordan schools. *International Education Studies, 3*(2), 211–218.

Benkler, Y. (2006). *The wealth of networks: How social production transforms markets and freedom.* New Haven, CT: Yale University Press.

Brogan, P. (2012). *Broadband and ICT ecosystem directly supports nearly 11 million high-paying U.S. jobs* (USTelecom Research Brief). Washington, DC: USTelecom. Retrieved from https://www.ustelecom.org/sites/default/files/documents/022812_Employment-Research-Brief-final.pdf

Brynjolfsson, E., & McAfee, A. (n.d.). *Race against the machine.* Retrieved from http://www.whitehouse.gov/sites/default/files/microsites/ostp/PCAST/PCAST_May3_Erik%20Brynjolfsson.pdf

Cairncross, F., & Cairncross, F. C. (2001). *The death of distance: How the communications revolution is changing our lives.* Boston, MA: Harvard Business Review Press.

Cisco. (2014a). *Cisco Visual Networking Index: 2013–2018 forecast Q&A.* Retrieved from http://www.cisco.com/c/en/us/solutions/collateral/service-provider/visual-networking-index-vni/qa_c67-482177.html

Cisco. (2014b). *Cisco Visual Networking Index: Forecast and Methodology, 2013–2018.* Retrieved from http://www.cisco.com/c/en/us/solutions/collateral/service-provider/ip-ngn-ip-next-generation-network/white_paper_c11-481360.pdf

Clark, P. (2013, August 13). Entrepreneurship education is hot. Too many get it wrong. *Business Week.* Retrieved from http://www.businessweek.com

ComScore. (2014). *2014 U.S. digital future in focus.* Retrieved from http://www.comscore.com/Insights/Presentations-and-Whitepapers/2014/2014-US-Digital-Future-in-Focus

Conlon, T. (2000). Visions of change: Information technology, education and postmodernism. *British Journal of Educational Technology, 31*(2), 109–116.

Cook, J. (2014, October 10). Hackers access at least 100,000 Snapchat photos and prepare to leak them, including underage nude pictures. *Business Insider.* Retrieved from http://www.businessinsider.com

de Vries, M. J. (2011). *Positioning technology education in the curriculum.* Rotterdam, Netherlands: Sense.

Editorial Projects in Education Research Center. (2011, September 1). Issues A–Z: Technology in education. *Education Week.* Retrieved from http://www.edweek.org

Fishbein, M., & Ajzen, I. (1975). *Belief, attitude, intention and behavior.* Reading, MA: Addison-Wesley.

Friedman, T. (2005). *The world is flat: A brief history of the twenty-first century.* New York, NY: Farrar, Straus and Giroux.

Gardner, H., & Davis, K. (2013). *The app generation: How today's youth navigate identity, intimacy, and imagination in a digital world.* New Haven, CT: Yale University Press.

George, D. S. (2014, April 23). High school students are all about computers but get little instruction in computer science. *Washington Post*.
Retrieved from http://www.washingtonpost.com

Glassman, C. F. (2009). *Brain drain: The breakthrough that will change your
life*. Mahwah, NJ: RTS.

Greenhow, C., & Robelia, B. (2009). Informal learning and identity formation in online social networks. *Learning, Media & Technology, 34*(2),
119–140.

Internet World Stats. (2014). *Internet usage statistics: The big picture: World
internet usage and 2014 population stats*. Retrieved from http://www
.internetworldstats.com/stats.htm

Krugman, P. (2013, June 13). Sympathy for the Luddites. *New York Times*.
Retrieved from http://www.nytimes.com

Lemke, C., Coughlin, E., & Reifsneider, D. (2009). *Technology in schools:
What the research says: An update*. Culver City, CA: Cisco. Retrieved
from   http://www.cisco.com/web/strategy/docs/education/tech_in_
schools_what_research_says.pdf

Lessig, L. (2000). *Code and other laws of cyberspace*. New York, NY: Basic
Books.

Lessig, L. (2006). *Code: Version 2.0*. New York, NY: Basic Books. Retrieved
from http://codev2.cc/download+remix/Lessig-Codev2.pdf

Loyland, B. (2014). *Stepping out of your comfort zone*. Retrieved from https://
www.zionandzion.com/stepping-out-of-your-comfort-zone

Luehrmann, A. (2002). "Should the computer teach the student . . ."—30
years later. *Contemporary Issues in Technology and Teacher Education*,
2(3). Retrieved from http://www.citejournal.org

Madden, M., Lenhart, A., Cortesi, S., Gasser, U., Duggan, M., Smith, A., &
Beaton, M. (2013). *Teens, social media, and privacy*. Retrieved from
http://www.pewinternet.org/2013/05/21/teens-social-media-and-
privacy

Manyika, J., Chui, M., Bughin, J., Dobbs, R., Bisson, R., & Marrs, A.
(2013). *Disruptive technologies: Advances that will transform life, business,
and the global economy*. McKinsey Global Institute. Retrieved from
http://www.mckinsey.com/insights/business_technology/disruptive_
technologies

McAfee. (2014). *Net losses: Estimating the global cost of cybercrime*. Santa
Clara, CA: Author. http://www.mcafee.com/us/resources/reports/rp-
economic-impact-cybercrime2.pdf

Missouri woman indicted in MySpace cyber-bullying case that ended in
teen's suicide. (2008, May 15). *Fox News*. Retrieved from http://www
.foxnews.com

National Cyber Security Alliance. (2013). *2013 NCSA/Raytheon Millennial
Cybersecurity Survey*. Retrieved from http://www.staysafeonline.org/
ncsam/resources/#sthash.QwuBgswt.dpuf

National School Boards Association. (2007). *Creating and connecting: Research and guidelines on online social—and educational—networking.* Alexandria, VA: Author. Retrieved from http://grunwald.com/pdfs/Grunwald_NSBA_Study_Kids_Social_Media.pdf

National School Boards Association. (2011). *Making progress: Rethinking state and school district policies concerning mobile technologies and social media.* Alexandria, VA: Author. Retrieved from http://www.nsba.org/sites/default/files/reports/MakingProgress.pdf

Pink, D. H. (2005). *A whole new mind: Moving from the information age to the conceptual age.* New York, NY: Penguin.

Project Tomorrow. (2014). *The new digital learning playbook: Understanding the spectrum of students' activities and aspirations.* Retrieved from http://www.tomorrow.org/speakup/SU13DigitalLearningPlaybook_Student Report.html

Purcell, K., Rainie, L., Heaps, A., Buchanan, J., Friedrich, L., Jacklin, A., . . . Zickuhr, K. (2012). *How teens do research in the digital world.* Retrieved from http://www.pewinternet.org/2012/11/01/how-teens-do-research-in-the-digital-world/

Rosen, D., & Nelson, C. (2008). Web 2.0: A new generation of learners and education. *Computers in the Schools, 25,* 211–225.

Sabizan, F., & Gilakjani, A. B. (2013). Teachers' attitudes about computer technology training, professional development, integration, experience, anxiety, and literacy in English language teaching and learning. *International Journal of Applied Science and Technology, 3*(1), 67–75.

Schneiderman, E. T. (2014, April 22). Taming the digital wild west. *New York Times.* Retrieved from http://www.nytimes.com

Shontell, A. (2014, May 2). 5 months after turning down billions, Snapchat's growth is still exploding with 700 million photos shared per day. *Business Insider.* Retrieved from http://www.businessinsider.com

Sidel, R. (2008, January 23). Cheer up, Ben: Your economy isn't as bad as this one. *Wall Street Journal.* Retrieved from http://online.wsj.com

Smith, C. (2014, April 2). US e-commerce growth is now far outpacing overall retail sales. *Business Insider.* Retrieved from http://www.businessinsider.com

Stoup, P. (2008). The development and failure of social norms in Second Life. *Duke Law Journal, 58,* 311–344.

Teen hackers: 10 stories of young code-crackers. (2012, July 18). *Huffington Post.* Retrieved from http://www.huffingtonpost.com

Toffler, A. (1984). *Future shock.* New York, NY: Bantam.

Total US retail sales top $4.5 trillion in 2013, outpace GDP growth. (2014, April 10). *eMarketer.* Retrieved from http://www.emarketer.com

Tubaishat, A. (2014). An investigation into the attitudes of nursing students toward technology. *Journal of Nursing Research, 22*(2), 119–125.

VeraQuest. (2013). *Teacher technology usage.* Retrieved from http://www
.edweek.org/media/teachertechusagesurveyresults.pdf

Wylie, S., & Marri, A. (2010). Teledeliberative democratic discourse: A case
study of high school students' use of Web 2.0. *Campus-Wide Information Systems, 27*(4), 193–209.

Yee, N., Bailenson, J. N., Urbanek, M., Chang, F., & Merget, D. (2007). The
unbearable likeness of being digital: The Persistence of nonverbal
social norms in online virtual environments. *Cyberpsychology &
Behavior, 10*(1), 115–121.

Zhao, Y. (2006, January 16). Creativity cannot be taught, but it can be
killed. *Detroit Free Press.*

CHAPTER FIVE

The Wrong Technology Implementation

Top Down Versus Bottom Up

TWO TECHNOLOGY PARADOXES

"Computers meet classroom; classroom wins." So said Larry Cuban in 1993. Even though computers were spreading swiftly at the time, Cuban believed that technology was used marginally in classrooms and the future of technology-driven school reform was clouded. Fast forward 20 years to 2013. Technology has become far more prevalent in public schools. Back in 1991, on average 18 students shared one computer in schools (Cuban, 1993). By 2009, the student-to-computer ratio had decreased substantially to 5:3 (National Center for Education Statistics, 2010). In 1991, schools were not wired, let alone equipped with gadgets such as tablets, SMARTboards, and smartphones. In 2009, 93% of U.S. classroom computers had Internet access, and 73% of teachers reported that their students used cell phones in the classroom or at home to complete assignments (Purcell, Heaps, Buchanan, & Friedrich, 2013).

While devices become more ubiquitous in schools, one of the paradoxes is that technology is still disproportionally underused or misused. According to a study on college students' use of online learning platforms where they can take courses, instructors and students use these platforms predominantly for repetitive tasks such as transmitting course materials (syllabus, readings, assignments) or posting announcements (Lonn & Teasley, 2009).

In addition to being underused, technology can be misused. A teacher from Omaha, Nebraska, writes on the National Educational Association Faculty Lounge blog that despite thousands of dollars spent on SMARTboards, some schools use them as giant TV screens (Force, 2013).

The paradox of oversold and underused/misused technology raises the question of *why?* Why has technology integration in schools unfolded in what Cuban (1993) called a snail-like pace despite all these years of efforts and investment in infrastructure, devices, and professional development? Answers such as insufficient funding, limited availability, teacher resistance, and inadequate administrative support seem plausible but insufficient to explain this paradox (Cuban, 1993; Ertmer, Ottenbreit-Leftwich, & York, 2006).

Another paradox is that technology is reportedly *overused* outside school despite being *underused* inside school. It is no secret that students nowadays use technology excessively, if not obsessively, outside of the classroom. American children are found to spend, on average, more time on mobile devices than sleeping (Rideout, Foehr, & Roberts, 2010). Both public survey and anecdotal observations suggest that students are quite "into" technologies and spending a great amount of time on mobile devices. And yet, when it comes to applying technology for school work, students often display less excitement and energy than they do on afterschool technology time.

This chapter will first examine these two paradoxes by comparing two existing modes of technology implementation: the before 3 p.m. model versus the after 3 p.m. model. It will also explore alternative ways to implement technology that might help teachers and students put technology to better use.

BEFORE 3 P.M. MODEL

Someville Elementary School[1] is a typical suburban public school with well-trained teachers, sufficient funds, and adequate administrative

---

1. For privacy purposes, the names used here are pseudonyms.

support for its technology literacy initiative. The school does not seem to have the most common issues that many technology integration programs suffer from (Becker, 2000), such as technology accessibility and teachers' competency with technology.

In the third-grade technology literacy (TL) classroom, the instructor, Mr. Smith, sits at the front of the classroom with a desktop computer in from of him, and his 20 students sit around five tables, each of which has a computer. Mr. Smith asks his students to go to his website, where he has spelled out the agenda of today's class: keyboarding practice. The following is Mr. Smith's direction for the activity:

> This week we will be working on keyboarding practice. Make sure you are keeping your fingers on the right keys! Remember . . . if I see your fingers in the wrong place, I'm going to move you back to an earlier stage! Try to look at the screen and not the keyboard when you are working on our BBC Typing game. When you are done with the game, please take a quiz on typing correctness. At the end of class, be sure to take a survey on your interest level on typing.

Clearly Mr. Smith is a caring teacher: He tries to engage his students with games. He cares about their interest level in the subject matter by asking students to take a survey. He prepares the lesson plan ahead of time and posts it on his homepage for easy access. Nevertheless, the classroom activity outlined by Mr. Smith's online directions is basically asking students to do exactly what their teacher tells them to do and to pass the teacher's test. Otherwise, they will be in "trouble." We consider this the *Before 3 p.m.* model, in which teachers implement technology in such a way that they control the "who, when, how, and why" of technology use in the classroom. In this model there are explicit learning objectives, instructions from teachers, tests ensuring that students achieve the learning objectives, and a great deal of teacher involvement.

AFTER 3 P.M. MODEL

In contrast to the Before 3 p.m. model, in the *After 3 p.m.* model of technology implementation there are no textbooks, no instructions from teachers, no testing, and very minimal instructor support. Despite all that, children cannot get enough of the technology that is in place.

One example that has recently gathered widespread attention is Minecraft, a game about breaking and placing blocks, according to the official website (minecraft.net). Think of Minecraft as a strategy game that combines the magic of Lego and Harry Potter simultaneously in a virtual world. Fascinating children all over the world, without giving explicit instructions, Minecraft allows children to figure out how to build and protect their secret garden or a dream lab in their own way. Despite the lack of instructions or tasks, the game works like magic in the eyes and minds of children. They chat with friends about Minecraft during school recesses, seek out YouTube videos to learn how experts on the other end of the world "do cool stuff" with Minecraft, gather on Wikispaces to exchange ideas, and fly around the house like zombies imagining they are still in the Minecraft world after their parents have to shut down their computers because they have already had too much Minecraft time in a day. It is that powerful and hypnotic.

Another example of the After 3 p.m. model is the "hole-in-the-wall" (HiW) experiment mentioned earlier in the book (Mitra, 2003). In this experiment, researchers led by Professor Sugata Mira used a rugged design to place a computer into an exterior wall so that the learning station could withstand tough outdoor conditions; this was done in two locations. By installing a proprietary power management system, the researchers could let children play on the computers in the wall unsupervised, with few downtime and maintenance needs. The researchers installed each computer with mini games and short videos in English so that children could pick up some new English vocabulary while playing with the computers. The computers had Internet access, so children could use the newly learned English words to search the Internet on their own. After deploying the learning stations in an Indian village, the researchers left and let children explore the computers on their own. The children were free to play with the computers and negotiate with their peers about a range of matters, such as turn taking and problem solving.

A month later, the children had taught themselves to use the computer and also picked up some skills in English and mathematics (Mitra et al., 2005). Because of its huge success, the model was implemented in various regions around the world, including India, South Africa, the United Kingdom, and Australia, and generated tremendous impact on local people's learning lives.[2]

What's interesting about the HiW experiments is that, if given appropriate free, public, and unsupervised access, underprivileged children can engage on their own in complex tasks such as digital literacy, language literacy, social interaction skills, problem solving, and research, regardless of their nationality, gender, language, ethnicity, and socioeconomic background (Mitra & Dangwal, 2010).

BEFORE 3 P.M. VERSUS AFTER 3 P.M.: WHAT ARE THE DIFFERENCES?

It should be pointed out that the above examples are heuristics of two contrasting ways of implementing technology. Needless to say, there are exceptional examples of technology being amazingly implemented in classrooms and adored by students, and there are lousy afterschool technology programs as well. The Before 3 p.m. model example mentioned earlier is a simplified case, and the two examples of the After 3 p.m. model are heuristics that suggest rather than define how technology should be implemented. In close examination of these examples, though, it becomes obvious that five sets of opposing qualities are at work that give both models distinctive appeal. These contrasting qualities may also partially account for the two paradoxes raised at the beginning of the chapter.

The Technology: Minimally Used Versus Optimally Used

The first difference between the two models is whether technology is used in an optimal way. In the Before 3 p.m. model, technology is employed mainly as a complementary tool to make the existing teaching practice more effective and efficient. Intentionally or unintentionally, the power of technology is minimized in this model. In the example from Mr. Smith's classroom, the computer is treated similar as a typewriter, but we know that computers can do more

---

2. See details of HiW's worldwide replication at www.hole-in-the-wall.com/newsevents.html.

than that. In contrast, technology in the After 3 p.m. model is used in a more imaginative way. In the HiW experiment, students figured out how to use the wired computer to watch simulations and search for relevant information, which are some of the most powerful and relevant functions of computer.

The Plan: External Curriculum Versus Internal Interest

From the planning perspective, the Before 3 p.m. model usually has a curriculum imposed by school districts or higher administrative institutions. Curriculum is the first priority to be fulfilled, rather than students' interests. The curriculum has well-defined learning objectives and standards, reflecting the knowledge and skills that students are supposed to master. The curriculum decides what is *the* correct way to use a piece of technology, even though in reality technology can be used in a variety of ways. Students may explore their own interests with technology in the Before 3 p.m. type of classroom, but they have to first fulfill all the learning objectives specified in the curriculum. In essence, it is the curriculum requirements rather than students' interests that are emphasized in this type of technology implementation.

The After 3 p.m. model cannot be more different than the Before 3 p.m. model in terms of curriculum and learning objectives. Minecraft, for example, has no objectives or ultimate tasks outlined for its players. But that does not stop players from spending hours creating "complicated stuff" in the game or chatting with fellow fans about various techniques in the game. The same can be said of the HiW experiment implemented in the Indian village. It is precisely the lack of explicit objectives determined by external parties that fascinates children. When external curriculum gives the stage back to students, they are liberated to pursue their own interests in the technology-empowered learning space. In one of the HiW experiments, the Indian children were fascinated by a video about DNA that they found using the computer station, and they wanted to learn more about DNA. Along the way, the children managed to collaborate with each other to accomplish several tasks within a short amount of time, such as mastering basic English vocabulary in biology and searching online for more information about DNA. The children negotiated about taking roles (e.g., those who are good with technology do the online searching, those who are good with vocabulary work on English words). They also negotiated about turn taking (who gets to use the computer at the moment and for how long, as the group only had two HiW stations to share). Without an external curriculum, children are free to take initiative and to explore their shared interests.

The Execution: Teacher-Driven Versus Student-Driven

The third difference between the two models has to do with the execution of learning. The Before 3 p.m. model is highly driven by teachers in terms of how technology is placed, used, and assessed in a classroom. As revealed by Mr. Smith's teaching plan in the earlier example, the computers in the classroom are supposed to be used only for typing in that session, rather than being used otherwise. In this model, students do not have much control of how they can use the computers. While it might be an efficient way for teachers to drive the learning process and meet benchmarks and standards, there are some serious side effects to this model. One downside is that students are unintentionally trained to be followers rather than leaders in their own studies. When teachers make more and more decisions for their students, the students will feel less and less the need to make decisions. Students growing up in this kind of environment might end up spending too much time studying and too little time thinking about what they are studying for.

In contrast, the After 3 p.m. model makes students the boss of their own learning processes. They have to take the lead because teachers are not around all the time to provide guidance. Students have to take ownership of their learning endeavors in this model. Over the past few decades, After 3 p.m. type of technology programs have been implemented in different subject matter areas, such as math (Cognition and Technology Group at Vanderbilt, 1992), reading (Zhao & Gillingham, 2002), diversity and technology skills (Cole, 1996), and digital storytelling (Lemke, Lecusay, Cole, & Michalchik, 2012). Although these programs vary by subject matter and student demographic profile, they have one element in common: Students take ownership of the learning process by making their own decisions about why, what, when, and how to learn with the aid of technology.

The Support: More Versus Less

The fourth difference lies in the amount of external support available in the technology-enhanced environment. In the Before 3 p.m. model, teachers provide more detailed instructions, make the learning materials more accessible, and provide more emotional support and conductive feedback. They test more often, ensuring that students grasp the skills or knowledge points that they are supposed to grasp. It is assumed that *more* is good, and more teacher intervention will automatically make students learn better.

Interestingly, one of the key features of the After 3 p.m. model exemplified by Minecraft and the HiW experiment is the *lack* of adult intervention. As a matter of fact, there are no formal learning tasks or objectives that learners have to do. There are no teachers nearby smiling, nodding, patting on their shoulders, and helping out all the time. The content is not readily accessible in the machine or game that students are playing with. The children actually have to expend extra effort to seek out whatever they need in order to solve the puzzle that they are interested in. In the HiW experiment, for instance, the Indian children were even willing to learn a new language (English) in order to read online articles on the topic that they were researching. In Minecraft, young players have to read pages and pages of online resources or watch long videos to figure out how to build a maze, even though the younger generation is often cast stereotypically as a generation of uninterested readers with short attention spans (Richtel, 2010). While the After 3 p.m. model diminishes adult intervention to a minimal level, it adds a few elements that sweeten the learning process: respect of students' interests, freedom to explore, faith in students' ability to achieve something meaningful (rather than underestimation of their ability). These elements are exactly the ones that are lacking in most of the Before 3 p.m. technology programs.

The User Reaction: Bypassing the Positives Versus Rationalizing the Negatives

The fifth difference between the two models concerns user experience, specifically, students' reaction to the two different technology environments. In the Before 3 p.m. model, it is not rare to have students overlook the instructions that their teachers have meticulously prepared. The excitement that students express about the learning tasks is not nearly as intensive as their teachers would have expected. As for adult support, students sometimes take it for granted or even shy from it, despite the amazing amount of support that the teachers are willing to offer. In short, for all the positive things that teachers try to provide, many students are politely overlooking them, if not declining them outright.

However, in the After 3 p.m. model, it is interesting to see students defend the model strongly by not only touting the positives but also rationalizing the negatives. Students admit that the lack of learning objectives might seem confusing at the beginning, but they quickly point out that's the empowering part—to have the freedom to explore and figuring out on one's own. They acknowledge the fact that not all information is conveniently provided to them, but they quickly point out that it is the search and exploration part that is special and memorable, similar to how one might go out of one's way to find a special edition of a music album. Students might confess that at the beginning it is a little scary to embark on the self-service type of learning, but later on they recall proudly that what they have accomplished together with their peers completely exceeded their own expectations. Even students sometimes underestimate themselves! In the HiW experiment, despite the language barriers, the Indian children apparently convinced themselves that it was worth their time and effort to play with a computer that displays things that they did not understand right away. As for games such as Minecraft, even though the interface seems blurry and primitive, children all over the world try to defend the game by explaining to their baffled parents that the game is so cool and fun and creative (Bilton, 2013).

ALTERNATIVE WAYS TO IMPLEMENT TECHNOLOGY

Based on the five contrasting qualities between two models of technology implementation, there are several alternative ways to conceive the role of technology and how it can be optimally implemented for promoting success and innovation.

Alternative 1: Unleash the True Strength of Technology

Technology is not omnipotent. Like human beings, technology can do certain jobs extremely well and certain jobs not so well. The key is to identify the strength of technology for each subject area and let technology do its job (Zhao, Hueyshan, & Mishra, 2000). Take writing, for example.

Recent anthropological studies of digitally inclined teenagers found that students consider school writing as an entirely different species from the writing that they do outside of school on social media websites (Ito et al., 2013). The writing skills taught in schools have traditionally focused on spelling, grammar, structure, and content. In outside-school writing, audience is the first and foremost element that students factor into their writing. Youngsters creatively employ different media and tools to attract the attention of their different audiences. In contrast, the audience in school writing is their teachers or whoever will grade their papers, which is rather abstract and inauthentic. In outside-school writing, communication and self-expression are the main purposes of writing, whereas in school writing, passing the test or meeting the standards set by adults is probably valued more than communicating something real and genuine. Therefore, there is an awkward disconnect between the kind of writing skills pursued in the school context and the kind of writing that students develop outside of school. This disconnect has caused quite a bit of struggle for both students and teachers in terms of figuring out what writing is for and what it means to be a good writer (Ito et al., 2013).

What are the distinct advantages that technology brings into the writing process? Maybe it's not the spellcheck feature that improves students' spelling skills. Maybe it's not that technology helps students type faster and neater. Maybe what really matters is technology's power to enable students to reach a vast and real audience that they could never dream of in the traditional classroom. In the traditional classroom, if a student writes an excellent essay, it might be passed around the classroom for peer admiration, or published in the school magazine, or maybe even receive a national award. But the student has to invest a lot of time and resources to publish something for a real audience, on top of being a really good writer. Publishing to a real audience was indeed a privilege for students living in an age without computers and the Internet. Nowadays, however, all students (or the vast majority) with the appropriate facilities can publish articles online if they want to. Not only can they publish to a large audience, but also they can receive feedback from the audience instantly. This is the real power of technology: helping students reach a large authentic audience.

Ironically, filters and other techniques still exist in some schools to purposefully disconnect school computers from cyberspace (Baron, 2014; Walthausen, 2014) or fence smart devices off the grid as mentioned in Chapter 2. Students in such schools cannot reach the kind of audience that they are supposed to be able to reach when using computers. When they use smart devices, they are still primarily talking to their classmates or their teachers, as they would do without technology. If the power of technology is suppressed rather than unleashed, no matter how "smart" the tablets and apps become, students will not benefit much from this technology in practicing writing or any other subject area, for that matter.

Alternative 2: Serving the Long Tail of Knowledge

Ken Robinson (2006) raises a thought-provoking question in a TED talk: "There isn't an education system on the planet that teaches dance every day to children the way we teach them mathematics. Why?" It is a longstanding way of life for schools to devote the most precious resources—staff time, technology, space, textbooks—to a small amount of premium knowledge that enables one to function in a human society, such as language and math. Technology is mainly deployed in schools to facilitate the pursuit and transfer of this type of premium mainstream knowledge. Therefore, a huge amount of knowledge has sadly been overlooked and underserved in schools.

The *Long Tail* theory provides another perspective on the distribution of knowledge and how technology can be deployed creatively to promote the diversity of knowledge that has been underserved by schools. Long Tail (also known as the 80/20 rule, the Pareto Curve, or the power law) refers to a distribution model of various social phenomena, whereby the 20% most frequently occurring events appear in the head of a distribution curve, and the 80% least frequently occurring ones show up in the long tail of the curve. The theory was developed 100 years ago by an Italian economist named Vilfredo Pareto to describe a relationship between population and income (20% of the population possesses 80% of the entire society's wealth). Since then, it has been applied to describe language, social, and other types of phenomena. Anderson (2006) popularized this idea more recently and extolled the power of technology to reach and serve underserved niche audiences extremely well by providing endless options.

Examining the knowledge of human society as a whole, a similar pattern of distribution curve exists as well, where the classics lie in the head and the unorthodox lies in the tail. Whatever knowledge lies in the head attracts much more attention, resources, and legitimacy than what lies in the tail does. That is exactly the reason why math receives far more instructional attention and resources than dancing does. This is how knowledge was treated in the past and is still being treated in many schools. The following real-life tale may give some colors to how technology could be implemented inside and outside of schools to serve the long tail of knowledge.

The Story of DJ Focus Kelvin Doe: The 15-Year-Old Lectures at Harvard

Kelvin Doe was born in Freetown, Sierra Leone (in West Africa), and grew up with very little technology. Electricity is considered a luxury in his hometown. Nonetheless, Doe had a fascination about technology, so deep that he went to the dustbins after school to retrieve electronic parts discarded by others. With the scrap electronics parts, he built his own radio station for his community and he became known as "DJ Focus" in his hometown. Because of his incredible ability to invent, Doe became a winner of Global Minimum's Innovate Salone 2012, traveled to the U.S., presented his inventions at MIT, and lectured to a group of undergraduate engineering students at Harvard College. In a YouTube video featuring his story (watched 5 million times), Kelvin Doe said to the camera, "I like the name DJ Focus, because if you focus, you'll succeed." (THNKR, 2012)

The gist of the story boils down to three points: (1) Never underestimate how long the tail of knowledge can be in terms of children's interests. In Doe's case, the dustbin and what's inside it became his muse, but this kind of thing is normally dismissed by adults and in schools. This is a real-life case of "others' trash is one's treasure." (2) Never underestimate students' power of will. When they find something close to their heart, children can become quite serious and focused. (3) Never define technology in a narrow and rigid way. With imagination, old and new technology alike can spark inspirational ideas in the minds of children.

Alternative 3: Designing a Space for Possibilities, Not for Predictions

Technology should be used to create a learning space—a breathable space that nurtures possibilities rather than merely fulfilling predictions. Often the technology-enhanced learning space is not as liberating as it is meant to be, because of the proliferation of instructions, options, and adult intervention. Indeed, students rationalize the negatives and defend the After 3 p.m. model, despite the lack of instructions and intervention from adults.

This paradox might be explained by a concept not so commonly discussed in the realm of education. The concept is called *empty space* in Chinese art. While technology implementation and art creation seem unrelated matters from two separate worlds, a well-designed technology programs should both make good scientific sense and embody excellent artistic taste. The concept of empty space in Chinese art may provide a fresh perspective for designing a learning space with technology. Empty space is a concept that originated in Daoism, and it has a significant impact on Chinese literature, music, calligraphy, and painting. According to the *Tao Te Ching*, it is the empty space inside of a cooking pot that makes the pot useful for cooking, and it is the emptiness within a piece of architecture that makes it a livable space (Lao Tse, 2008, Ch. 11). Empty space is regarded as the beginning of the myriad things. As the art critic Weimin He (2005) notes, "The very charm in Chinese literature lies where it is without words; in music, where it is soundless conveys more than sound . . . so the very absence of content can itself create rhythm and consonance."

The power of emptiness is embodied in the After 3 p.m. model examples described earlier. It is reflected in the element of minimal adult intervention, which the HiW researchers consider one of the defining factors that makes their program so successful. Likewise, it

> Technology should be used to create a learning space—a breathable space that nurtures possibilities rather than merely fulfilling predictions.

is precisely because Minecraft does not force an explicit task on its players that numerous possibilities are felt, perceived, and explored enthusiastically by them. In other words, it is not as terrible an idea as adults tend to believe if the designer sweetens the technology learning space with a certain degree of indulgence—allowing students some time to play with the machines, to try some of their "silly" ideas, to have fun, and to have the opportunity to be surprised by how much they can accomplish with technology.

CONCLUSION

The reasons are not so difficult to pin down now if we revisit the two paradoxes raised at the beginning of the chapter: (1) oversold and underused computers in schools and (2) technology being underused inside school versus overused outside school.

Technology is underused because technology use in school celebrates teachers' teaching rather than students' interests. Technology is really in the hands of teachers and administrators, rather than in those of students. When students surrender to various requirements and restrictions on technology, also surrendered are their interests in it.

Technology is used more extensively after school than in school because students find real audience in afterschool technology environments, because they find a real outlet for their creativity, and because they find some kind of freedom—freedom to follow their interests, freedom to pursue niche knowledge that is dismissed by schools, freedom to learn from failures, and freedom to find their own voices.

REFERENCES

Anderson, C. (2006). *The long tail: Why the future of business is selling less of more.* New York, NY: Hyperion.

Baron, K. (2014, June 16). What's the impact of overzealous Internet filtering in schools? *MindShift.* Retrieved from http://blogs.kqed.org

Becker, H. J. (2000, January). *Findings from the teaching, learning, and computing survey: Is Larry Cuban right?* Paper presented at the School Technology Leadership Conference of the Council of Chief State School Officers, Washington, DC.

Bilton, N. (2013, September 15). Disruptions: Minecraft, an obsession and an educational tool. *New York Times.* Retrieved from http://www.nytimes.com

Cognition and Technology Group at Vanderbilt. (1992). The Jasper experiment: An exploration of issues in learning and instructional design. *Educational Technology Research and Development, 40,* 65–80.

Cole, M. (1996). *Culture in mind.* Cambridge, MA: Harvard University Press.

Cuban, L. (1993). Computer meet classroom: Classroom wins. *Teachers College Record, 95*(2), 185–210.

Ertmer, P. A., Ottenbreit-Leftwich, A., & York, C. (2006). Exemplary technology-using teachers: Perceptions of factors influencing success. *Journal of Computing in Teacher Education, 23*(2), 55–61.

Force, R. (2013). *Do Smartboards make smart students?* Retrieved from http://www.nea.org/home/40355.htm

He, W. (2005). *The mystery of empty space.* Retrieved from http://www.heweimin.org/Texts/mystery_of_empty_space.pdf

Ito, M., Gutierrez, K., Livingstone, S., Penuel, B., Rhodes, J., Salen, K., . . . Watkins, S. C. (2013). *Connected learning: An agenda for research and design.* Irvine, CA: Digital Media and Learning Research Hub. Retrieved from http://dmlhub.net/wp-content/uploads/files/Connected_Learning_report.pdf

Lao Tse. (2008). *Tao te ching.* Shanghai, China: Zhong Hua Shu Ju.

Lemke, J., Lecusay, R., Cole, M., & Michalchik, V. (2012). *Documenting and assessing learning in informal and media-rich environments.* Retrieved from http://lchc.ucsd.edu/MacArthur-Learning-Report_2012-12.pdf

Lonn, S., & Teasley, S. D. (2009). Saving time or innovating practice: Investigating perceptions and uses of learning management systems. *Computers & Education, 53,* 686–694.

Mitra, S. (2003). Minimally invasive education: A progress report on the "hole-in-the-wall" experiments. *British Journal of Educational Technology, 34,* 367–371.

Mitra, S., & Dangwal, R. (2010). Limits to self-organising systems of learning: The Kalikuppam experiment. *British Journal of Educational Technology, 41,* 672–688.

Mitra, S., Dangwal, R., Chatterjee, S., Jha, S., Bisht, R. S., & Kapur, P. (2005). Acquisition of computer literacy on shared public computers: Children and the "hole in the wall." *Australasian Journal of Educational Technology, 21,* 407–426.

National Center for Education Statistics. (2010). Teachers' use of educational technology in U.S. public schools: 2009 (NCES 2010-040). Retrieved from http://nces.ed.gov/pubsearch/pubsinfo.asp?pubid=20 10040

Purcell, K., Heaps, A., Buchanan, J., & Friedrich, L. (2013). *How teachers are using technology at home and in their classrooms.* Retrieved from http://pewinternet.org/Reports/2013/Teachers-and-technology

Richtel, M. (2010, November 21). Growing up digital, wired for distraction. *New York Times.* Retrieved from http://www.nytimes.com

Rideout, V. J., Foehr, U. G., & Roberts, D. F. (2010). *Generation M2: Media in the Lives of 8- to 18-Year-Olds: A Kaiser Family Foundation Study.* Menlo Park, CA: Henry J. Kaiser Family Foundation. Retrieved from http://www.kff.org/entmedia/upload/8010.pdf

Robinson, K. (2006). *How schools kill creativity.* Retrieved from http://www.ted.com/talks/ken_robinson_says_schools_kill_creativity?language=en

THNKR. (2012). *15-yr-old Kelvin Doe wows M.I.T.* Retrieved from https://www.youtube.com/watch?v=XOLOLrUBRBY

Walthausen, A. (2014, February 14). Schools should be teaching kids how to use the Internet well. *The Atlantic.* Retrieved from http://www.theatlantic.com

Zhao, Y., & Gillingham, M. (2002). Ingredients of successful after-school programs: The experience of KLICK. In R. Garner, Y. Zhao, & M. Gillingham (Eds.), *Hanging out: Community-based after-school programs for children.* Westport, CT: Greenwood Press.

Zhao, Y., Hueyshan, S., & Mishra, T. P. (2000). Teaching and learning: Whose computer is it? *Journal of Adolescent & Adult Literacy, 44,* 348–354.

CHAPTER SIX

Making It Right

Reimagining Education in the Second Machine Age

The history of applying technology in education is not one with glorious victories. Quite the contrary, it is filled with cycles of ambitious claims and costly failures. None of the technological innovations that once inspired great enthusiasm succeeded in delivering the promised transformation or even significant improvement in education over the past hundred years. From Thomas Edison's films to radio and television, from B. F. Skinner's teaching machine to computerized learning systems such as PLATO, from Seymour Papert's LOGO to interactive Hyperstudio, and from multimedia laserdiscs to multimedia computers, all once were thought to have the potential to drastically change how education was organized and delivered. But today, the institutional structure of education remains pretty much the same as it was 100 years ago, so do students' school experiences. Technology has failed even to alter the most basic element of education—the classroom. "When technology meets classroom, classroom wins" was the conclusion reached by Stanford education historian Larry Cuban more than 20 years ago (Cuban, 1993).

About the same time that Cuban penned his pessimistic conclusion about the fate of technology in education, the visionary MIT mathematician and pioneer in innovative use of computers in education Seymour Papert (1993) said that "thinking about the future of education demands a similar labor of imagination" as that required to see "the birth of the industry that would lead to the jumbo jet and space shuttle" in the 59-second flight of Wilbur and Orville Wright in 1903 (p. 29). "The prevalent literal-minded, 'what you see is what you get' approach measuring the effectiveness of computers in learning by the achievements in present-day classrooms makes it certain that tomorrow will always be the prisoner of yesterday," wrote Papert in his seminal book *The Children's Machine: Rethinking School in the Age of the Computer* (p. 29). He likened judging the value of computers based on classroom achievement to

> attaching a jet engine to an old-fashioned wagon to see whether it will help the horses. Most probably it would frighten the animals and shake the wagon to pieces, "proving" that jet technology is actually harmful to the enhancement of transportation. (p. 29)

Papert (1993) wrote the book to "stir the imagination to invent alternatives" in education (p. 34). But unfortunately the kind of imagination he hoped to stir has yet to occur. Much of the efforts to use technology in education over the past two decades have been "attaching a jet engine to an old-fashioned wagon." While technology has become more powerful beyond what most would have imagined in 1993, the prevalent mindset remains the same: using technology to improve the traditional paradigm of education.

Technology is not the only innovation that has failed to revolutionize education. Numerous other educational innovations failed as much as technology. Progressive education, the Dalton plan, the Montessori method, the Reggio Emilia approach, Democratic education, and Waldorf education are just a few of the better known examples of efforts that once promised to revolutionize education over the past 100 years (Tyack & Cuban, 1995). These innovations were supposed to reshape schools into more child-centered educational institutions, to transform what David Tyack and William Tobin (1994) call "the grammar of schooling": "the regular structures and rules that organize the work of instruction . . . for example, standardized organizational practices in dividing time and space, classifying students and allocating them to classrooms, and splintering knowledge into 'subjects'" (p. 454). But today, schools operate virtually the same way as they did 100 years ago, with students grouped by age, managed by an adult teacher, in physical classrooms, following a uniform curriculum, and studying for fixed time periods dedicated to each subject. While the innovative ideas have not died completely, they exist only on the periphery.

There are many reasons why innovations fail. Timing is critical. Quite often an innovation fails to take root not because it is a bad idea or lacks the right strategy but because it is introduced at the wrong time, that is, when there is no widespread recognized need for the innovation, when the innovation is not well developed enough to be a noticeably better alternative to the existing arrangement, or when the innovation lacks associated infrastructure to support its expansion. For example, while the videophone concept was developed in the late 1800s and various forms of videophones were developed throughout the 20th century, none of the innovations succeeded. The technologically brilliant AT&T's Picturephone was a commercial disaster in the 1970s. Instead of a hundred thousand users expected by AT&T, it had only several hundred subscribers. It was not until the arrival of the 21st century when videophone applications such as Skype became accepted as a common way of communication.

It took more than 100 years for videophone technology to reach the tipping point to revolutionize human communication. But the videophone did not just wait for 100 years. It took active research and development efforts and experienced many failures along the way. As a result, the technology gradually matured. In the meantime, supporting infrastructure such as digital and networking technology became more sophisticated and the need for video-based distance communication became more salient as businesses became more distributed across distance and humans moved around more frequently.

Historically speaking, the failure of an innovative idea at a certain time does not mean it won't work in the future. More important, for innovations, especially transformative ones, to succeed at a revolutionary magnitude, failure is a necessary experience. It points to new directions, inspires new efforts, and breeds new solutions. Failure is an essential element of the evolutionary process that leads to a revolution.

In this sense, all previous efforts to apply technology to improving education and reforms to change the grammar of schooling were failures when judged at the time, within a short historical time frame. But in the long run, they are necessary trials and errors and sources of lessons for improvement that will eventually culminate into a grand revolution.

Has the time arrived for revolutionizing education? Is it time to take more seriously the challenge of reimagining education and reinventing a new grammar of schooling? If so, what would the new grammar look like? This chapter attempts to answer these questions by analyzing how technological changes have created the need for reinventing the basic elements of schooling: the what, how, and where of learning. This chapter concludes with a framework for the new school enabled by new technologies.

THE NEED FOR REIMAGINING EDUCATION

The traditional grammar of schooling is largely responsible for the mistakes we have documented in this book. In the traditional paradigm, education is equated with schooling. And schooling is about imparting prescribed curriculum in students. Teachers are the exclusive agents responsible for the task of ensuring that prescribed knowledge and skills are effectively transmitted to students. The primary place for the transmission is the classroom. Technology has been used primarily to improve this paradigm without reimagining the what, where, and how of education. It has been typically considered as an aid to improve the mastery of prescribed curriculum, thus the *what* of learning remains the same. As a result, the measure of the benefit or impact of technology on learning remains students' performance on tests of prescribed skills and knowledge. In terms of the *where* of education, it remains in the physical classroom with enhanced technological equipment such as interactive whiteboards, networked computers, and mobile devices. Students still learn as a group from the teacher, who determines when and how the technological devices shall be used. The *how* of education continues as before with the teacher as the authority of knowledge who transmits knowledge to students with the assistance of technology.

Attaching a jet engine to a horse-drawn wagon is unlikely to prove the power of jet engines. Similarly, adding modern technology to the traditional paradigm of education is unlikely to realize the potential of that technology. More important, to meet the challenges brought about by technology, education must go through fundamental transformations. Education has always been in a race with technology (Goldin & Katz, 2008). Technological inventions and innovations created by a few have always continuously caused changes to society, some more drastically than others. These changes create new industries, new business models, new ways to conduct our daily life, and new possibilities as well as new problems, while making old ways of doing things obsolete. Education, the institution charged with the responsibility to prepare competent citizens for society, has always needed to ensure that future generations are equipped with the appropriate capabilities consistent with societal demands.

Education is always in "catch up" mode in that it needs to anticipate what society might look like in the future due to technological changes and respond with appropriate actions. Luckily, revolutionary technological transformations have not happened very often in human history. Technological revolutions resulting in fundamental redefinition of the value of knowledge, skills, and talents have been even less frequent, thus allowing education to catch up. But today we are in the midst of a major societal transformation brought about by digital technology (Brynjolfsson & McAfee, 2014). This wave of transformation has redefined the value of skills, knowledge, and talents and will continue to do so. Education must respond to this redefinition if it is to prepare competent citizens for the "second machine age."

REIMAGINING THE WHAT: CURRICULUM

Curriculum has been one of the essential elements of schooling. It defines the *what* of student learning. Following the grammar of traditional schooling, all students are supposed to master the same content and skills prescribed by an authoritative body, be it a national or local government agency or a widely accepted nongovernmental credentialing organization. Such prescriptions stipulate the scope and sequence of learning for all children. They represent the expectation of what all children should know and be able to do at a certain age. They dictate educational activities offered by a school and the organizational structures of instruction in schools.

Reimagine What's Worth Learning: The Need

A primary function of such a curriculum is to define worthwhile qualities students should develop through schooling. Schools are supposed to equip children with the qualities deemed necessary or desirable for successful adult life in a society, while eliminating or suppressing undesirable ones. Humans vary in terms of aptitudes, interests, and passions. The innate variations are amplified by the environment and experience. Consequently, when children arrive at school, they vary a great deal. But not all abilities, interests, or passions are believed to be of equal value or desirability in a given society. Thus it is necessary to have an authoritative body to define worthwhile qualities for all students as a guide for school activities so that schools can focus on teaching the worthwhile and stemming the undesirable.

Massive societal changes brought about by technological advancement have rendered the traditional functions of a preset uniform curriculum obsolete. First, given the rapidity of social changes, it is no longer possible to predetermine what knowledge and skills will be valuable in the future (Zhao, 2012). New jobs replace old ones constantly as old industries disappear thanks to technological changes and globalization, which makes existing jobs move around the globe. For example, according to a report of the Kauffman Foundation, existing firms in the United States lost on average over one million jobs annually from 1977 to 2005, while an average of three million jobs were created annually by new firms (Kane, 2010). As a result, there is no sure way to predict what jobs our children will have to take in the future. The head of PISA, Andreas Schleicher (n.d.), recently said: "Schools have to prepare students for jobs that have not yet been created, technologies that have not yet been invented and problems that we don't know will arise" (para. 8). If one does not know what careers there will be in the future, it is difficult, if not impossible, to prescribe the knowledge and skills that will make today's students ready for them.

Second, it is also unnecessary to prescribe "worthwhile" knowledge and skills anymore. Societies have arrived at an age when all talents are valuable and all skills and knowledge are worthwhile. Thanks to increased productivity, many human beings have accumulated much wealth and command more time for leisure activities that enable them to consume more psychological and spiritual products and services, which rely on traditionally undervalued talents and skills. For example, best-selling author Daniel Pink (2006) makes the case for the rise of the traditionally undervalued right brain–directed skills in *A Whole New Mind: Why Right Brainers Will Rule the Future*. Economist Richard Florida (2012) points out the value of creativity in his book *The Rise of the Creative Class*. Furthermore, numerous research reports assert the value of noncognitive skills such as grit, social skills, and a growth mindset (Brunello & Schlotter, 2010; Duckworth, Peterson, Matthews, & Kelly, 2007; Dweck, 2008).

Third, the traditional conception of curriculum works against the development of talents and skills needed in the new society. The traditional curriculum was designed to prepare a workforce for the industrial age when the majority of jobs required similar skills and knowledge. Thus the curriculum favors a narrow band of cognitive skills such as quantitative skills, verbal skills, and logic skills and focuses on a narrow set of disciplines such as math, language arts, and sciences. However, traditional jobs that require routine procedural knowledge and skills have been increasingly displaced by sophisticated technology (Brynjolfsson & McAfee, 2014) or offshored to places where such skills can be acquired at a lower cost (Friedman, 2007).

Education thus has to equip future generations with the skills that cannot be replaced by machines or offshored (Barber, Donnelly, & Rizvi, 2012; Wagner, 2012; Zhao, 2012). These skills include creativity, entrepreneurial thinking, global competencies, and noncognitive skills that have been generally referred to as 21st century skills. These skills are generally missing in the traditional curriculum. Moreover, the traditional curriculum, in its attempt to ensure all students master similar sets of skills, attempts to fix children's deficits according to external standards instead of supporting their passion and strength. As a result, children are rarely given the opportunity to be challenged to develop their strengths and interests into great talents needed in the age of creativity and in a society that needs great entrepreneurs to create jobs and opportunities (Malone, Laubacher, & Johns, 2011; Zhao, 2012).

Reimagine What's Worth Learning: The Possibility

A preset curriculum has also been considered necessary because schools do not have all the resources to meet the needs of all students. Traditionally, learning opportunities and resources have often been limited to what is available in a school. As a result, regardless of the wealth and size of a given school, it is indeed virtually impossible for any school to provide an education that meets the individual needs of all students. Schools therefore must choose to allocate their resources to certain domains. To do so, they need a curriculum to help them decide what to include.

The unprecedented availability of learning resources made possible by technology has made it unnecessary to prescribe a uniform educational experience for all students. The advancement in information and communication technologies over the past decade or so has made human knowledge and experts universally accessible. The omnipresence of constantly connected, interactive, and multimedia devices enables anytime access to libraries, museums, science labs, design studios, TV and radio programs, newspapers and magazines, as well as millions of potential experts around the world. Schools no longer monopolize learning opportunities. Neither should they. Consequently, while students still attend school, schools are not solely responsible for providing all learning opportunities students need. In other words, schools no longer need a preset curriculum to guide its allocation of resources.

Reimagine What's Worth Learning: Personalized Curriculum

Technology has made it both necessary and possible to reimagine one of the most untouchable elements of traditional schooling: the curriculum. In contrast to the traditional one-size-fits-all education dictated by externally prescribed curricula, we could imagine education as a personalized experience that supports the development of interests and strengths of each child. What's worth learning is determined by the child rather than by external bodies. It is whatever provides the best opportunity for individual students to pursue their passions and enhance their strengths.

A personalized curriculum is an expanded version of *emergent curriculum* (Jones, 2012; Jones & Nimmo, 1994). Originating from the Reggio Emilia approach, the emergent curriculum is a way of planning curriculum. An emergent curriculum is negotiated between individual students and their teachers based on students' interests, passions, and strengths. Emergent curriculum has historically been applied to curriculum planning in early childhood education, when children are typically not placed in specialized classes and taught by one or two teachers. Personalized curriculum can be viewed as emergent curriculum for older children, who negotiate and collaborate with the school to come up with a learning experience that capitalizes on their strengths and supports their interests.

To realize personalized learning, the role of the school is transformed from enforcing a prescribed curriculum to empowering and enabling each child to craft an individualized curriculum. The school does not dictate to students a uniform pathway. Instead, it responds to students' needs. Course offerings are generally based on careful observation and thoughtful reflections on students' interests, passions, and abilities. Schools are encouraged to offer a broad range of opportunities for students to "play" with their interests and strengths, to discover their passion, to find out their weaknesses and strengths, and to spark unknown interests. Schools should also be flexible and responsive so as to encourage students to take risks, to change course, and to admit mistakes. This does not mean, however, that students are allowed to do whatever they like, when they like. Quite the contrary, schools should hold students accountable for their choices. Schools should challenge students to aim high, to be disciplined, and to persevere.

Personalized education transfers the ownership of learning to students. In other words, it is the students who are responsible for deciding what they wish to learn. Students become owners of their own learning enterprises and thus must actively seek to construct their own learning pathways. Just like an active visitor to a museum, the student decides which path to follow, which exhibition to see and how much time to spend on it, and which seminars to attend.

To realize personalized education, schools need to go through some structural transformations. For example, the century-old practice of grouping students by biological age needs to be abolished, as does the practice of allocating students into classes of similar sizes. Students can elect to attend lectures, participate in discussion groups, and join working teams that reflect their interests and abilities. In the same spirit, schools no longer need to operate classes for a fixed period time, for instance, 45 minutes for 20 weeks. Classes can be offered depending on the content, topic, and needs. Some can be as short as 2 weeks and some can be as long as 3 years. Likewise, schools could devote entire days to one topic for a certain period of time.

In summary, a personalized curriculum, made necessary and possible by technology, requires a vision for schools. A school that aims to provide personalized education is conceptually not one school, but many schools on one campus. Each student has his or her own unique school experience.

REIMAGINING THE HOW: PEDAGOGY

Like curriculum, pedagogy is another element of the traditional grammar of schooling that has persisted despite numerous efforts to introduce more innovative ways of teaching. The mainstream practice of teaching has remained teacher-centered. Teachers continue to dominate the process of learning as the authority of knowledge and manager of the classroom. Direct instruction continues be the favored method of teaching. The primary goal of teaching is to transmit knowledge, to help students master, understand, or memorize prescribed content.

Within the traditional paradigm of pedagogy, students are treated as passive recipients of instruction. Their role is to follow the teacher, to master what the teacher wants them to master, and to demonstrate that they have mastered it in the way the teacher wants. Put another way, the students are mostly consumers, and consumers who have to prove that they are good at consuming. The process of learning from the student perspective is to receive information, consume it, and give it back to the teacher. The goal of learning is about finding answers and giving them back to the teacher properly.

A more fitting metaphor of the traditional pedagogy is managing a factory of mechanical workers, where the teacher is the manager and students the workers. The teacher gives instructions and assigns tasks to students each day. The students work as hard as possible to finish the tasks. At the end of the work period, the students are rewarded or punished based on how well they have complied with the instructions and completed the tasks.

Reimagine Pedagogy: The Need

For decades, the traditional pedagogy has been challenged. John Dewey, Maria Montessori, Helen Parkhurst, A. S. Neil, and other advocates for a child-centered approach to education raised questions about the autocratic, command-control, teacher-centered pedagogy. The advent of constructivism and social cultural theories led by psychologists such as Jean Piaget (1957) and Lev Vygotsky (1978) contributed scientific evidence against the traditional pedagogy. More recently, brain research and psychological studies have supplied even more evidence to show the traditional pedagogy goes against the nature of learning and human development (Bransford, Brown, & Cocking, 2000; Brown, 1994; Medina, 2008). Moreover, "a large and growing body of literature supports the proposition that active student engagement in the learning process produces higher quality learning than the traditional lecture and testing approaches used in the United States" (Mascolo, 2009, p. 7).

The quality of learning is indeed one of the primary reasons for the call to transform the traditional pedagogical paradigm, which has been found to lead to lower levels of student engagement, superficial processing of content, rote memorization of information, and a loss of intrinsic motivation, in comparison to student-centered pedagogy (Lambert & McCombs, 2000; Watson & Reigeluth, 2008). It also leads to the suppressing of individual students' interests, lowering aspirations, limiting possibilities to explore, and failing to develop higher order thinking skills due to the tightly controlled and well-scripted nature of traditional teaching.

The problems with the traditional pedagogical paradigm have become more pronounced due to the development of technology. One of the most damaging aspects of the paradigm is its effectiveness in instilling the consumer and employee mindset. The traditional pedagogy favors compliance, rewards compliance, and values acquisition of existing knowledge. It is effective in imparting prescribed knowledge and fostering skills to solve known problems in well-defined domains. But it does little in cultivating the entrepreneurial and creative mindset required to discover problems worth solving, to chart new paths in unknown and unpredictable situations, or to take ownership and the risk for generating novel solutions to challenging problems. In the traditional paradigm, students are rarely engaged in creating authentic products that serve a purpose. For their entire career as students, they are mostly engaged in artificial exercises and produce artifacts to demonstrate their mastery of the content. As a result, they seldom are encouraged to consider their responsibilities for solving real problems or to exercise their creativity and imagination.

Technology, as discussed before, has made the world more unpredictable. It has also replaced jobs that require routine knowledge and skills with ones that require entrepreneurial thinking, creativity, and innovation skills.

Reimagine Pedagogy: The Possibility

One reason for the failure of earlier efforts to transform the traditional teacher-centered pedagogy into one that is student-centered is the general lack of easy access to knowledge and experts. Up until recently, teachers have been the only source of knowledge, aside from print publications. Schools have been the few places dedicated to offering access to a collection of knowledge and experts. Thus even if a school or a teacher wished to make learning more student-centered, it would have been difficult, if not impossible, for students to learn things that the teacher did not know or the school was not equipped to provide. Likewise, even if students wished to learn something, they had difficulty finding sources of information and experts if these sources were not immediately available in the school.

Today, as previously discussed, technology has drastically alleviated the access issue. Globally networked information and communication devices and applications enable ubiquitous access to virtually the entire body of human knowledge, most of which has been digitized. Cloud computing, social networks, online media and databases, digital books and other publications, and multimedia productions have broken the monopoly of information by teachers and schools. Students have in their possession the potential to learn anything from anyone at any time.

Reimagine Pedagogy: Product-Oriented Learning

It is apparent that the traditional teacher-centered pedagogy needs to be changed. It is also more feasible than ever before to make the change. The change is more than piecemeal tinkering. It is a paradigm shift, a complete rethinking of how teaching and learning are carried out (Papert, 1993; Watson & Reigeluth, 2008; Zhao, 2012). The shift requires efforts to reimagine all aspects of teaching and learning: from teacher-centered to learner-centered, from knowledge transmission to talent development, and from information consumption to product creating.

Product-oriented learning (POL) is one of the many proposed frameworks that represent the paradigm shift. First proposed by Yong Zhao (2012) in his book *World Class Learners: Educating Creative and Entrepreneurial Students*, POL is a version of project-based learning (PBL), an innovative approach that has gained traction in education in recent years. POL is a more dramatic departure from the traditional pedagogy than PBL, which in practice has often been teacher-directed and constrained by a uniform curriculum.

POL has a number of essential characteristics that represent an entirely different pedagogy from the traditional one. The goal of POL is to create authentic products or services. That is, the learning is to serve a genuine need, either that of the learner or of others. The need can be the learner's strong desire to create a product of self-expression, for instance, a piece of art, a novel, a poem, or a musical performance. The need can also be a genuine interest in advancing knowledge in a discipline, solving a scientific or social problem. Furthermore, the need can be identifying opportunities to help better other people's lives or improve the world in general.

This product orientation changes the nature of learning from consumption to creation. Learning is no longer the act of consuming what the teacher or curriculum wants to teach, but the process of acquiring knowledge and developing skills to create products or services to serve genuine purposes. It goes way beyond learning by doing or learning by making. It is learning to do, learning to make, learning to discover, and learning to serve.

POL thus starts with the learner's interests and passions, rather than the curriculum or teacher. Stemming from his or her interests, the learner proposes to address a need, be it personal or social or scientific. The learner then conducts research (learning) to justify to the teacher or other authority such as the school or parents that the need is genuine. This need-driven learning helps the learner understand the purpose of learning, exercise responsibility for learning, and practice social-emotional skills such as empathy and sympathy—all important attributes for productive, creative, and entrepreneurial citizens.

POL helps the learner discover his or her strengths and weaknesses and understand individual differences. After the learner identifies a need to address, he or she is asked to propose a solution, which should be both distinctive and feasible. To do so, the learner needs to examine his or her own abilities, identify available resources, and explore his or her perceived interests and strengths.

POL emphasizes the quality of the outcome created by the learner in addition to the degree to which the outcome meets a genuine need. Thus in POL, students are held accountable to produce products of the highest quality, judged by their intended users, teachers, and or experts instead of by standardized tests. It thus requires students to engage in a process of sustained and disciplined revisions and improvements. Through this process, students learn to develop a growth mindset, solicit and respond to feedback, and practice the important skills of self-examination and critical thinking.

POL encourages—in fact forces—students to actively seek collaboration because a product or service that serves a genuine need often requires talents, skills, and resources beyond what one individual can possess. To create a high-quality product or service requires teamwork by a group of individuals with diverse skills and interests. The process is inherently collaborative and takes advantage of the diversity naturally in existence in human beings. More important, it teaches students the value of diversity and respect for differences.

In summary, POL is a response to the need to reimagine pedagogy in response to the need for talents that cannot be replaced by technology and the possibility of ubiquitous access to knowledge created by technology. It is also a response to the reality that human society is going through another revolutionary transformation akin to the Industrial Revolution. One consequence of this transformation is that people can participate in authentic social and economic activities from a very young age, like in the Agricultural Age. The Industrial Revolution located economic activities away from homes and communities, separating the workplace from the living place. Thus education has been viewed as a way to prepare children to enter the workplace, to live an adult life. Today, technology has enabled people to work from home, to reach a global market from one's home, and to develop meaningful products and services at a very young age. Thus it is possible to realize the idea that education is not simply preparation for life; education is life itself.

REIMAGINING THE TEACHER-MACHINE RELATIONSHIP: SUMMARY

Will this round of technological innovations and investment in education break the former cycles of hope and disappointment? The answer is unknown, but from what we have learned from the past, a major determinant will be how well we have learned our lessons and how seriously we take the task of reimagining how education is organized in the face of rapid technology development.

So far, we have discussed how technology has created the need and possibility for reimagining curriculum and pedagogy. The reimagined curriculum and pedagogy can begin to be implemented only when the relationship between human teachers and technology can be realigned.

"Never send a human to do a machine's job," a statement uttered by Agent Smith in the movie *The Matrix,* is good advice for us to reimagine the relationship between humans and technology in education. Technology is developed to extend or replace human capacities. It is designed to do things that human beings are unable or unwilling to do or do things more efficiently than human beings, either more effectively or at lower costs. By design, technology is meant to replace certain human abilities. In other words, if technology can do certain things better with more efficiency or even things that are impossible for humans to do, we should let technology do it. There is no reason for humans to compete with machines. As a result, technology has replaced human beings entirely in cases where human involvement is straightforward and simple. For example, ATMs have replaced certain banking jobs and robotics has replaced certain manufacturing jobs.

Education is much more complex than depositing a check or getting cash from a bank teller. It is fundamentally a human endeavor. Technology will probably never be able to replace human teachers entirely. But many tasks that have traditionally been performed by human teachers can and should be done by technology so as to free human teachers to do things that machines cannot do or do as well. In other words, technology can make education more human if used properly.

To better capitalize on the potential of technology, schools and teachers need to reimagine the relationship between technology and human educators so as to determine what can be delegated to technology and what must be done by human educators, or can be done better by them. The reimagining can happen at multiple levels, and how it looks depends on student characteristics, present arrangements and resources, grade levels, and educational objectives. But the advice would be the same: Never send a human to do a machine's job. To paraphrase, we should not send human educators to do things that technology can do more effectively or at lower costs, and we should certainly allow technology to do things that human teachers cannot do or are unwilling to do.

A realigned teacher-machine relationship is essential for realizing the reimagined paradigm of schooling. As previously discussed, a personalized curriculum and product-oriented pedagogy requires schools to transform from one-size-fits-all factories into personal learning ecosystems. In a personal learning ecosystem, learners pursue their interests, create meaningful products, and take on the responsibility for their own learning. To realize this transformation, schools have to provide a lot more resources and opportunities and rethink how to organize and develop them. The increase in demand for resources and opportunities cannot possibly be met by human teachers alone. Thus schools will need to rely on technology, but not use it to replace human teachers. Instead, technology is meant to expand human capacities.

An essential element of the learning ecosystem is social and emotional support and personal guidance so that individual learners are properly challenged, supported, and mentored on their personal learning journey. No technology, even so-called big data, can be as socially and emotionally engaging to the human learner as another human being. No technology can understand the psychological conditions of an individual human learner, nor can it interpret human purposes. No technology can have the same level of wisdom, intuition, and caring as a human teacher. Thus emotional and social support, as well as mentoring, can be achieved only by human teachers.

However, no human being can compete with Google in terms of how much information one can hold and give access to. No single human can present information in engaging and multimedia ways that rival the computer, nor can one single human store as much information as banks of data servers. Additionally, no human teacher can be as patient as a machine when dealing with repetitive mechanical tasks.

Thus human teachers should withdraw from such tasks as information gathering, storing, and transmission, as well as tasks as mechanical exercises.

After all, there is no reason for teachers to compete with Google or YouTube!

REFERENCES

Barber, M., Donnelly, K., & Rizvi, S. (2012). *Oceans of innovation: The Atlantic, the Pacific, global leadership and the future of education.* London, UK: Institute for Public Policy Research.

Bransford, J. D., Brown, A. L., & Cocking, R. R. (Eds.). (2000). *How people learn: Brain, mind, experience, and school.* Washington, DC: National Academies Press.

Brown, A. L. (1994). The advancement of learning. *Educational Researcher, 23*(8), 4–12.

Brunello, G., & Schlotter, M. (2010). *The effect of non cognitive skills and personality traits on labour market outcomes.* Munich, Germany: European Expert Network on Economics of Education.

Brynjolfsson, E., & McAfee, A. (2014). *The second machine age: Work, progress, and prosperity in a time of brilliant technologies.* New York, NY: W. W. Norton.

Cuban, L. (1993). Computers meet classroom: Classroom wins. *Teachers College Record, 95*(2), 185–210.

Duckworth, A. L., Peterson, C., Matthews, M. D., & Kelly, D. R. (2007). Grit: Perseverance and passion for long-term goals. *Journal of Personality and Social Psychology, 92,* 1087–1101.

Dweck, C. S. (2008). *Mindset: The new psychology of success.* New York, NY: Ballantine Books.

Florida, R. (2012). *The rise of the creative class.* New York, NY: Basic Books.

Friedman, T. L. (2007). *The world is flat: A brief history of the twenty-first century.* New York, NY: Farrar, Straus and Giroux.

Goldin, C., & Katz, L. F. (2008). *The race between education and technology.* Cambridge, MA: Harvard University Press.

Jones, E. (2012, March). The emergence of emergent curriculum. *Young Children,* pp. 66–68.

Jones, E., & Nimmo, J. (1994). *Emergent curriculum.* Washington, DC: National Association for the Education of Young Children.

Kane, T. (2010). *The importance of startups in job creation and job destruction.* Kansas City, MO: Kauffman Foundation.

Lambert, N., & McCombs, B. (2000). Introduction: Learner-centered schools and classrooms as a direction for school reform. In N. Lambert

& B. McCombs (Eds.), *How students learn* (pp. 1–15). Washington, DC: American Psychological Association.

Malone, T. W., Laubacher, R. J., & Johns, T. (2011, July–August). The big idea: The age of hyperspecialization. *Harvard Business Review*, pp. 1–11.

Mascolo, M. F. (2009). Beyond student-centered and teacher-centered pedagogy: Teaching and learning as guided participation. *Pedagogy and the Human Sciences, 1*(1), 3–27.

Medina, J. (2008). *Brain rules: 12 principles for surviving and thriving at work, home, and school.* Seattle, WA: Pear Press.

Papert, S. (1993). *The children's machine: Rethinking school in the age of the computer.* New York, NY: Basic Books.

Piaget, J. (1957). *Construction of reality in the child.* London, UK: Routledge & Kegan Paul.

Pink, D. (2006). *A whole new mind: Why right brainers will rule the future.* New York, NY: Penguin.

Schleicher, A. (n.d.). *The case for 21st-century learning.* Retrieved from http://www.oecd.org/general/thecasefor21st-centurylearning.htm

Tyack, D., & Cuban, L. (1995). *Tinkering toward utopia: A century of public school reform.* Cambridge, MA: Harvard University Press.

Tyack, D., & Tobin, W. (1994). The "grammar" of schooling: Why has it been so hard to change? *American Educational Research Journal, 31*, 453–479.

Vygotsky, L. S. (1978). *Mind in society: The development of higher psychological processes.* Cambridge, MA: Harvard University Press.

Wagner, T. (2012). *Creating innovators: The making of young people who will change the world.* New York, NY: Scribner.

Watson, S. L., & Reigeluth, C. M. (2008, September/October). The learner-centered paradigm of education. *Educational Technology*, pp. 42–48.

Zhao, Y. (2012). *World class learners: Educating creative and entrepreneurial students.* Thousand Oaks, CA: Corwin.

Index

A SAGE Company

CORWIN HAS ONE MISSION: to enhance education through intentional professional learning.

We build long-term relationships with our authors, educators, clients, and associations who partner with us to develop and continuously improve the best evidence-based practices that establish and support lifelong learning.